The Choice

The Choice:

Evolution or Extinction?

A Thinking Person's Guide
to Global Issues

ERVIN LASZLO

A Jeremy P. Tarcher/Putnam Book
published by
G. P. Putnam's Sons
New York

A Jeremy P. Tarcher/Putnam Book
Published by G. P. Putnam's Sons
Publishers Since 1838
200 Madison Avenue
New York, NY 10016

Charts on pages 23, 40, 43, 44, 47, 124, 147, and 159 courtesy of Hans-Wolff
Graf, "Deutsches Bundesverband für Steuer-, Finanz-, und Sozialpolitik
(DBSFS) e.V., and Anthropos e.V. für die Kinder dieser Welt, München."

Published simultaneously in Canada

Library of Congress Cataloging-in-Publication Data

Laszlo, Ervin, date
     The choice, evolution or extinction? a thinking person's guide
to global issues.
         p.   cm.
     Includes bibliographical references and index.
         ISBN 0-87477-753-4
     1. Environmentalism.   2. Environmental responsibility.
3. Sustainable development   I. Title.
GE195.L38   1994
363.7—dc20   93-29994 CIP

Design by Lee Fukui

Cover design by Mauna Eichner

Cover illustration © by Joel Nakamura

Printed in the United States of America
1   2   3   4   5   6   7   8   9   10

This book is printed on recycled paper.

Contents

Introduction

We are but one among a multitude of living things on a small planet that is swimming in the endless space of a vast galaxy within an almost infinite cosmos. Yet surely we are among the most astonishing products of evolution in the universe. As atoms form from particles, and molecules form from atoms, so crystals and cells form from molecules, and a breathtaking variety of organic species form from cells. The human species, too, formed in the course of this grand evolutionary development, co-evolving in a delicately balanced rhythm with the embracing web of life on our planet. After 15 billion years of evolution in the cosmos and 4 billion years of evolution on Earth, in the last 100,000 years the vast processes of evolution brought forth the phenomenon of human life and consciousness. But, in the span of the last few decades, the future of the human species, and with it the continuation of evolution on this planet, has been placed in serious jeopardy.

In the closing years of the twentieth century, our world has become unsustainable. The classical empires of Babylonia, Egypt, China, and India endured for thousands of years. But the industrial societies that first emerged in Europe and North America are not more than a few centuries old, and they are not likely to be sustainable for much longer. Progressive environmental degradation and excessive levels of resource exploitation go hand in hand with mounting unemployment and rising criminality, economic and social polarization, and ethnic strife. For our societies to develop, and for their members to survive, a crucial choice must now be made—a choice that will decide whether we head for further evolution or final extinction. A continuation of the present trends would place in jeopardy the future of industrial societies, as well as the future of all life on Earth.

Our generation is called upon to make the choice that will decide our ultimate destiny. If we fail to make the right choice at the right time, our generation, or the generation of our children, will be the last in history. And if we and our children disappear, the untold potential for insight, creativity, love, and compassion of which the human spirit is capable will vanish from the stage of cosmic history. Never has the biblical message had such trenchant meaning as it has today: "Where there is no vision, the people perish."

We are forced to choose, for the processes we have initiated in our lifetime cannot continue in the lifetime of our children. Whatever we do either creates the framework for continuing the supreme adventure of life and consciousness on this planet, or sets the stage for its termination. The choice before us is urgent and important: It can be neither postponed nor ignored.

This challenge is unprecedented in history. In centuries past, even as a tribe or a village overreached itself and destroyed the integrity of its immediate environment, its people could move on, seeking virgin territories and fresh resources. Today, planet Earth as a whole is the new frontier. Our settlements are spreading throughout its habitable regions, and we live close to the outer bounds of its carrying capacity. Unlike in the past, our predicament is not local: It affects the entire system of life in the biosphere. There are no more islands, protected backyards where one can do as one pleases; what one person, one society does today affects many and perhaps all other persons and societies. In consequence, as one people or society overreaches the limits of its resources and its environment, its denuded lands and polluted waters endanger the planet's entire life-support system. Living within a crowded and delicately balanced economic, social, and ecologic system, we have become vitally dependent on one another and on our shared planetary habitat. If we overstress our environment, we can only head for another planet; on Earth there will be no place left for us to go.

Meeting the challenge of our times is difficult but not impossible. The remarkable faculties of a conscious mind embrace the powers of reason and intelligence, of love and solidarity. If we grow conscious of our condition, if we recognize the choice facing us, I believe that we shall not face extinction; we shall develop the insight and the will to opt for a life-enhancing path of evolution.

I

The Threat
to Survival

I

Where We Are Headed: The Grand Transition

May you live in interesting times.
CHINESE MALEDICTION

In the last decade of the twentieth century we have reached a crucial juncture in our history. We are transiting into a new kind of world that is as different from the world we leave behind as the grasslands were from the caves, and settled villages from life in nomadic tribes. Today we are growing out of the nationally based industrial societies that we created at the dawn of the first industrial revolution, and heading toward the interconnected, information-based, global socioeconomic system that emerges under the impact of new technologies and new individual, social, and economic opportunities.

Living in the midst of a grand transition is an unusual adventure, far different from the slower pace of change in previous epochs. Today, anyone who has reached mid-life will have witnessed the aftermath of a world war, the coming of age of the communication and information revolution, and the replacement of the cold war battle of two superpowers with a multipolar world led by the economy and marked by intense competition for information, technologies, and markets.

Patterns of life have seldom changed as significantly as this in any single lifetime. And, as in China for the last 5,000 years and Russia for the past five, when they did change, they brought upheaval and violence. But for most of us change is not necessarily violent, and wishing it on others is not necessarily a curse. Day after day new scientific discoveries are curing our diseases, extending our lifespan, helping us to reduce working hours and increase leisure time, permitting us to access and process a staggering amount of information, and enabling us to travel anywhere on the six continents in considerable comfort and safety.

A decade or two ago, most of us thought that science would create a veritable paradise on earth. The smashing of the atom would release cheap energy in abundance; the Pill would limit population growth; computers and automation would do all dirty, dangerous, and heavy work in factories and on the land; television would bring education into every home; and telecommunications would link all people on the globe. And once people were freed from dull, stultifying, and dangerous work they would become enlightened and considerate of one another. A new and better age would dawn, hallmarked by humanism, solidarity, and well-being for everyone.

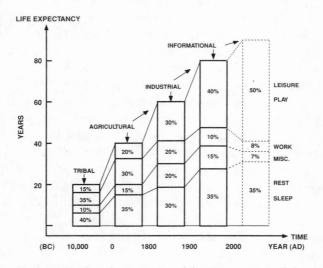

The historical and extrapolated future increase of the portion of a lifetime spent in leisure and play, compared to work, miscellaneous activities, and rest and sleep (values under optimum conditions).

Of course, such an age did not dawn, and there is increasing uncertainty as to whether or not it ever will. Yet the knowledge to achieve a significant level of health and well-being is there, even if people do not (for often they cannot) make adequate use of it.

As it is, life expectancy is increasing, and most of us enjoy greater comfort and more time for play, recreation, or reflection.

There are, however, two sides to this picture. Science and technology have raised human living standards for millions beyond all expectations, but social inequities, political stresses, and unreflective uses of technology have polarized humanity and degraded nature. They are creating problems of planetary dimensions. Global warming; the attenuation of the ozone shield; the menace of deforestation and desertification; the destruction of many species of flora and fauna; the extensive pollution of air, water, and soil; and the poisoning of the food chain are threats that all of us share.

There is no consensus yet on how to tackle these and other emergent problems. The world undergoing the grand transition is too new and its complexity is too high. We have not yet come to view it correctly, let alone manage it.

In the late twentieth century the world is indeed new: Classical assumptions concerning the nature of social and political reality have collapsed. We no longer live in an arena for the struggle of capitalism and communism led by two superpowers; it is a more complex world, a game with more players. The U.S.S.R. has disappeared, and the United States is preoccupied with economic problems at home. Japan holds on to prominence, and the "little dragons" of Asia are eager to follow suit. Europe has become a major economic power with its post-1992 single market and an already functioning East-West economic area of more than 380 million people. Many parts of the third world—more than 130 countries—sink further and further into poverty and underdevelopment. And environmental degradation shifts from a marginal issue to the center stage of international politics and world business.

Crisis always implies danger as well as opportunity. If the dangers of our own crisis are to be averted and its opportunities seized, we need to do at least two things: First, we need to better understand our world and its transition—what drives it, how it came about, and where it is headed. Second, we need to explore the practical options at our command to ensure our future. These are the imperatives of our survival, but they are not imperatives that anyone forces us to follow. The choice remains ours; we should not hesitate to take the positive option.

THE DRIVERS OF THE GRAND TRANSITION

Let us take the positive option and look at these survival imperatives in turn. The first questions we must ask are: What drives the current transition? How did it originate? Where is it headed?

A bird's-eye view of the processes that shape our world discloses an interesting picture. Two features stand out above all: "informatization," the rapid and progressive domination of information in life and society; and "globalization," the rapid and progressive globalization of the structures within which people and societies pursue their information-imbued activities.

THE INFORMATIZATION OF LIFE AND SOCIETY

One of the basic features of the current epoch of transition is the growing presence, and indeed prevalence, of information. The importance of information—knowledge, know-how, data, and the elaboration of data—has grown exponentially in all sectors and segments of society. In the past, societies were shaped mainly by the information processed in human brains. This was the case in raising children, creating businesses, setting up local or national governments, organizing churches or armies, and founding schools or theaters. But in the twentieth century the information processed in human brains has been increasingly supplemented by the information processed in technical systems. In the last decade of this century, advanced societies have become thoroughly "informated." They are no longer merely social, socioeconomic, and sociocultural systems; they are also *information-processing* systems.

Informatization Yesterday. The systematic use of information began in early antiquity. The number system, perhaps the greatest of all information-processing innovations, and some remarkable calculating devices such as the abacus, were invented thousands of years ago. However, machines that would significantly improve human calculating powers by executing operations through built-in programs were built only in the modern age. In 1642 Blaise Pascal invented an adding machine that may have been the first automated digital calculator; in 1671 Leibniz created an instrument that multiplied by repeatedly adding; and in 1833 Babbage produced the Analytical Engine, creating a logistical basis for building genuine computing machines.

About 100 years ago information-processing technologies took off. Herman Hollerith succeeded in the automation of the U.S. census count at the end of the nineteenth century, and Bell invented the telephone. At around the same time, Hertz developed the principle of wireless communication and pioneered the development of radio. Konrad Zuse built his Z_1, Z_2, and Z_3 computers in the 1930s, and Eckert, Mauchly, and Goldstein created the cumbersome but already accomplished ENIAC computer in 1946. UNIVAC I, a vast machine with 5,000 heat-generating vacuum tubes taking up an area of 220 square feet and weighing 5 tons, was used in 1952 to predict the landslide victory of Dwight D. Eisenhower. It made a sensation on national television.

The mid-century invention of the computational architecture of digital data-processing by mathematician John von Neumann permitted a quantum leap in electronic information processing. Through digitalization, numbers, letters, words, sounds, images, and the measurement of mechanical and electrical instruments could be rapidly and accurately transformed into strings of electronic pulses. Digital signal-processing computers benefited from the concurrent mass production of transistors for hearing aids and radios and became commercially available in the early 1950s.

Computers entered the field of production in the 1960s. CIM (computer-integrated manufacturing) harnessed the powers of the digital computer to integrate the different elements of manufacturing, so that the entire process could be operated as a single system. By virtue of the unique capabilities of the computer, this system could be flexibly automated and operated on-line, in real time.

During the 1970s computers became widespread thanks to the availability of mass-produced desktop units and workstations. Households and offices could no longer be without the ubiquitous small screen and keyboard. Then in the 1980s the power of earlier mainframe systems was compressed into full-fledged personal computers, and similar capabilities were further compressed into laptop and then palmtop computers. Now even trains and planes are populated with people busily punching their minikeyboards and gazing into their miniscreens.

In the 1980s managers of major manufacturing enterprises became aware of the competitive advantage of overall automation, optimization, and integration in a total-system process of manufacturing. Leading-edge industries began to encompass in computer integration not only the technological elements of the manufacturing system—product design, production planning and control, and shop-floor automation—but also such managerial elements as strategic planning, finance, human resources, and marketing. By 1990 the computer-integrated manufacturing enterprise had come of age. Companies like Toyota managed to build complex products such as automobiles almost entirely through the use of robots, directed and supervised by flexibly programmed computers.

Informatization Today. Today individual computers are increasingly interconnected through a variety of networking methods and technologies. Distributed computing environments allow individuals to reach out from their personal and portable computers to electronic networks, data banks, and mainframe computers. Thousands of complex operations have been programmed into computers as algorithms and into the sophisticated heuristics of artificial intelligence.

In all sectors of society such previously brain-based tasks as communication, calculation, and even pattern recognition are rapidly transferred to computers. Information processing systems have become deeply embedded in the structures of society and interact with them in countless ways. They are also becoming increasingly autonomous. The vast networks made possible by the technologies of information storage and elaboration in distributed computing and communicational environments do not require (and sometimes do not even allow) operational intervention by humans. International banks and financial institutions have almost completely delegated their accounting procedures and financial computations to fully automated programs, interfaced with globe-circling communication networks. Often, along with increasingly complex tasks, actual control is transferred to computers.

Automated computer systems are thoroughly integrated in manufacturing (CIM), design (CAD), and inventory control (Just-in-Time systems). They perform essential functions for the military (Early Warning and remote sensing systems), telecommunications (communication satellites), ground and air transportation (automatic rail switching systems, auto-pilots, and instrument landing systems), and in such complex operations as balancing the atomic chain reactions of nuclear power stations. The systems have become all but indispensable. They cannot be substituted by human brains, nor can they be "switched off" without inducing dramatic consequences that range from stock market chaos to nuclear meltdown. It is estimated that in Germany alone it would take 7 million persons to carry out the computational workload of the automated banking system.

Information has also become the crucial factor in channeling flows of capital. The information standard has replaced the gold standard as the basis for international finance. Worldwide communications enable and ensure that money moves anywhere around the globe in answer to the latest information—or misinformation.

Computers are getting more and more sophisticated: They are steadily climbing the ladder of human skills. Earlier devices replaced mainly lower-level skills, such as addition and subtraction, and the simpler forms of man-machine communication. With the advent of CIM and CAD, computers moved into slots that were previously the preserve of human technicians. And sophisticated programs, such as Automatic Theorem Proving (ATP) in mathematics, and the automatic sequencers used, for example, in the Human Genome Project (the international research project aimed at decoding the full set of instructions that make the human body) encroach on the skills of scientific specialists. The rapid growth of many kinds of expert systems during the last five years suggests that computers will continue to climb the ladder of human skills, even if, unlike Star Trek's Mr. Data, they are unlikely to match the still uniquely human qualities of imagination and creativity.

The market for computers—palmtops, laptops, desktops, workstations, minis, superminis, mainframes, and supers—attained more than $220 billion by 1991. It employs an ever larger segment of the work force. The effects of informatization are felt beyond the microelectronics industry itself: The sectoral distribution of the entire work force is becoming slanted toward the information area. Employment patterns have been shifting not only from agriculture toward industry, but even within industry from raw-material and energy-intensive branches toward information-intensive ones.

In the United States, the largest single work force in 1860 was still in agriculture; the information sector comprised a modest 5 percent. Between 1906 and 1960 the industrial work force became dominant, peaking in 1946 with 40 percent of the total employment. In the 1950s, however, the proportion of the work force in traditional industry began to decline, falling to 25 percent by the 1970s. At the same time, the segment of the work force employed in the information sector began a rapid rise, reaching about 50 percent of the total employment figure by the late 1980s. The primary and secondary information sectors taken together (that is, the set of people directly concerned with the production, processing, and transmission of information, together with those who are less directly involved with information processing, for example, in business management, accounting, clerical work, and market information services) also account for some 50 percent of the U.S. GNP.

Informatization Tomorrow. For the past several years there has been an estimated 10 percent annual decrease in size of system per unit of performance, and another 10 percent decrease in cost, and the learning curve does not show signs of leveling off. More and more information processing systems are coming on-line each year. In 1985 there were about 400 million microprocessors in use worldwide, incorporated in some 4 million computers and various command systems, household appliances, and electronically steered devices. This number grew to 3 *billion* in 1991. Currently, experts foresee a total of 10 billion microprocessors in worldwide use by the year 2000. At that point the number of artificial computing devices would exceed the number of natural computing devices—that is, human brains.

The systems coming on-line are more and more powerful. In 1985 about 1 million components could be integrated on a chip. By 1990 the number grew to 5 billion. Some predictions call for chips with 1 trillion components by the year 2000.

A new nervous system is being created in contemporary societies. This system is "exosomatic": It operates outside the human organism and is not limited by the cranium, which can

accept just so many brain cells. The artificial information processing system has almost infinite growth potentials, with its
bounds given only by the minimum size beyond which there is
noise or cross talk among electrons, and the maximum quantity of data held by a chip. And even these limits are expand-
able through optical processors and holographic data storage.
In principle, pulsed semiconductor lasers can transmit 10^{10}
bits of information per second (the information content of the
entire *Encyclopaedia Britannica* comes to about 10^{11} bits—
optical pulses could transmit it anywhere on earth in 10 seconds). In turn, a one-inch square hologram has nearly 100 million resolvable spots available for recording. This allows some
10,000 light sources to be linked up with 10,000 light sensors,
a recording magnitude well beyond the absolute physical capacity of chips. Moreover, holograms, like chips, can be su-
perposed and act as three-dimensional storage media rather
than as two-dimensional surfaces. In principle, a hologram the
size of a cube of sugar could store the entire contents of the
U.S. Library of Congress, handling some 1 trillion possible
interconnections among 1 million optical elements.

The linkage capacities of the new information processing
system are practically unbounded: Microprocessors can be
connected with high-capacity storage media and also can be
interconnected in communication networks of almost unlimited extension and density. The 3 billion microprocessors and
500 million telephones in service today are only the advance
guard of an integrated globe-girdling system such as the ISDN
(Integrated Services Digital Network). Such systems can be
switched into networks of automated data processing and
can transmit data as well as voice quasi-instantaneously the
world over.

The potential capacity of the new telecommunication systems is mind-boggling. To appreciate its dimensions, one can
best compare it with messages transmitted by humans. A liter-
ate individual who speaks and writes a relatively large number
of words every day produces a total "message unit" of approx-

imately 650 million words in a lifetime. An integrated world-wide telecommunication system operating at 100 gigabits per second and relayed by six space satellites could transmit the total annual message units of humanity in about four weeks—that is, it could carry in twenty-eight days flat all the words spoken and written by five and a half billion people during a period of 365 days.

Capacity of this kind will not necessarily mean overkill and waste: The excess capacity could be used to carry machine-generated messages. As it is, machine-generated messages are increasing at a far more rapid rate than the flow of messages generated by humans.

The exosomatic nervous system evolving in the contemporary world integrates machines and humans within complex feedback loops. It elaborates, stores, and transmits information in ways that are far more permanent and of several dimensions larger than the information flow that any but the most ardent science-fiction fan has ever dreamed of.

GLOBALIZATION IN GOVERNMENT

Another driver of the current transition is the progressive globalization of the institutions and structures of contemporary society. Globalization and informatization are organically related. The exponentially growing networks of information and communication prompt the creation of international and transnational networks and associations, and these in turn lead to the formation of more formal and permanent organizational structures. As a result, the vast flows of information that circulate around the globe have given birth to thousands of international and intergovernmental organizations. These, while they often create giant bureaucracies with questionable efficiency, are needed to coordinate and supervise processes that could be dangerous to our personal and national security or our individual and collective health.

Decisions implemented solely within the context of a nation's sovereign territories become increasingly ineffective: They do not make adequate inroads on an increasing number of problems and difficulties. Thus, slowly but apparently irreversibly the public sector is feeling its way toward the global arena. Even though the governments of nation-states are legally as well as politically bound to maintain the sovereignty of their people and their territories, they are reaching out beyond their borders in order to conclude a variety of arrangements and pacts with other actors, in the public as well as in the private sector. This has produced a plethora of economic and military alliances, global markets, and world-level accords and conventions.

The globalization of government has been growing apace with the decline of its power within the domestic arena. Prior to World War II, using methods that were dictatorial in the East and juridical in the West, the governments of the major powers controlled as much of the social and economic life of their countries as they deemed necessary. Even in the postwar decades, the governments of the United States and some countries of Western Europe, and of all the socialist bloc, had no difficulty in determining the direction of technological advance and dominating trade and finance as well. But in recent decades the governments even of the major powers became awash in a sea of interdependence. During the early phases of the cold war, the United States and the U.S.S.R. had to compete vigorously with each other for military superiority and global economic and political clout. Today they have to compete not only with each other, but also with Japan, Europe, the newly industrialized countries of Asia, and before long, China.

By now, monetary, trade, and investment issues have become intertwined and complex; the world economy is nearly ungovernable. Based on national power centers, more governance means more regulation and greater restrictions. A heavy governmental presence would only exacerbate economic and social inequities and create market distortions. Production on the international scale escapes national control and, except in the armaments and space sectors, so does technological progress. The rise of Japan, the integration and dramatically changed situation in Europe, and the continuing series of crises in Africa, Latin America, and the Middle East confront national governments with policy problems that do not respond to classical solutions.

Although agreement on ways to tackle the majority of the emerging transnational problems is still lacking, there is a new consensus on the need to join forces in tackling them. There is almost universal agreement, for example, regarding such classical objectives as the achievement of international peace and the abolishment of colonization. During the 1960s these time-honored goals were joined by others, such as sheltering international refugees, combating the spread of drugs and terrorism, and providing basic nutritional, educational, and health resources for children. Then, in the 1970s and eighties the protection of the environment and the management of the "global commons" (the oceans, the atmosphere, Antarctica, and outer space) became recognized global policy issues. Still more recently, the management of the volatile world financial system joined the roster of issues calling for global-level decisions.

Apart from humanitarian actions aimed at children and refugees, and police actions dedicated to combating drugs and terrorism, the areas where the new consensus on the need for joint action is moving governments toward the global dimensions are:

the maintenance of international peace and security;

the protection of the planetary environment; and

the regulation of the world financial system.

Peace and Security. Matters of peace and security are increasingly beyond the control of national governments. Even superpower security is becoming a transnational issue. Since

President Clinton's administration took office, more and more people in Washington have questioned the belief that assuring a high level of U.S. national security calls for assuming the role of the world's policeman, and bearing the burden of the high level of military preparedness that must go with it. Entrusting international peacekeeping to an international peacekeeping force may be a promising alternative.

The dilemma of the United States, the remaining global superpower, is not resolved. But the position of medium-sized and smaller countries is becoming clearer by the day. The emerging insight is that their national borders can be more effectively, and certainly more efficiently, safeguarded by a regional defense system than by a national army. This view is increasingly operational in Europe. A European Defense Community, rejected by France when it was first proposed in the 1960s, was revived in the 1980s in the guise of joint peacekeeping arrangements in the framework of the CSCE (Conference on Security and Cooperation in Europe). It is currently moving toward realization as a European Defense Force, a joint army whose establishment is slowed only by the complexity of its ties with NATO. An important step toward overcoming this problem was taken in May 1992, when France and Germany signed a protocol for creating a common defense force that other European states have since joined.

In Europe, most states are awakening to the realization that it is pointless for them to maintain an expensive army when with much smaller expenditures they can have an adequate joint security system. Even in Switzerland, where the army is a national institution that always has been highly respected by the population, the people had second thoughts about maintaining a costly defense establishment: In a 1990 referendum, almost a third of the respondents opted for abolishing the armed forces.

Since the demonstration of the effectiveness of collective peacekeeping in the Persian Gulf in 1991 and the insertion of the blue berets in Somalia and Bosnia in 1993, governments the world over began to look with fresh interest on international peacekeeping arrangements. In the past, UN peacekeeping forces have proved their effectiveness in hot spots such as Cyprus, and the Near and the Middle East. In 1988 they were honored with the Nobel Peace Prize. Despite frequent criticism of their effectiveness, support for UN forces is growing rapidly, not in the least because economic problems force the reduction of national military budgets, while security problems continue to plague most governments.

The Protection of the Environment. In the area of environmental protection, global action and decision-making have become imperative. World-level governance is most likely to come on-line first in the area of the global commons. The world's oceans and atmosphere, outer space, and polar regions are obvious domains of globally coordinated action. On the one hand, they cannot be readily divided, appropriated, and nationally or privately owned, and on the other, their integrity remains a precondition of ensuring humanly favorable conditions in the biosphere. Conventions for protecting extraterritorial waters, safeguarding the chemical composition of gases in the atmosphere, protecting and regulating the use of outer space, and maintaining the integrity of the ecology of the Antarctic already have been signed, and many more are in preparation.

As to environments that fall *within* the borders of nation-states, protection remains primarily the responsibility of national governments. An increasing number of them are experimenting with regulations to control ecological impacts. Environmental ministries have been created in most European countries and in several extra-European states as well, and the green parties are acquiring influence. But effective action is seldom possible within a purely domestic framework, and national measures are rapidly turning transnational. The EC countries are joining forces in creating a European Environmental Agency to coordinate the policies of member states.

Logically, the creation of a global-level institution must be the next step. There is a movement in this direction, although it is still beset with political and financial obstacles. In April 1990 agreement was reached in The Hague on the need for setting up an international high authority to create a binding policy framework with effective regulatory powers for both territorial and extraterritorial measures. But at the June 1992 World Conference on Environment and Development—the Rio "Earth Summit"—U.S. election-year politics prevented the Bush administration from signing protocols that other industrial nations such as Germany and Japan signed, not to mention entering into negotiation on the creation of a global environmental authority. Though the Clinton administration subsequently signed the treaty on biodiversity, the principal tangible result of UNCED, the Rio summit, was the creation of a string of commissions and advisory groups. Some, like the World Bank–led Global Environmental Facility (GEF), have potentially important financial clout. Others are mainly political talk forums, such as the UN General Assembly–mandated Commission on Sustainable Development (UNCSD). Hopeful new executive agencies include the UN Development Program–directed "Capacity 21" program, a smaller Sustainable Development Networks (SDN) fund, and an independent monitoring body, the "Earth Council" in Costa Rica.

The current plethora of global-level mechanisms faces a series of challenges, including the question of funding by the major powers and support by the internally divided 1,420-strong nongovernmental organizations that have registered with UNCED. These challenges will have to be met in short order: The global environment continues to deteriorate, and the need for an effective world-level authority is becoming each day more urgent.

The Financial System. Of the three domains where governance is becoming globalized, the area of world finance is the most recent. Not surprisingly, the governance of this system is also the most embryonic. However, like a viable embryo, global financial system regulation is growing rapidly. Governments are becoming aware that, just as by themselves they cannot protect their citizens from concerted external aggression and cannot shield their people from the effects of environmental degradation, they are also unable to protect their national economies from the harmful effects of unfavorable and unpredictable financial flows. The occasional summits of a few heads of government, and the ad hoc caucuses of some heads of central banks, are far from adequate for this task. Finance, like security and the environment, knows no national borders and responds to no unilateral national measures—or to poorly orchestrated international initiatives.

Until the 1990s, the very idea that a sector or dimension of the world economic system should require public governance was controversial: Past attempts at regulating the world economy ended in failure. This was the case in regard to the "new

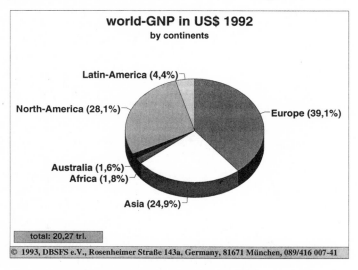

The share of the continents in the world's Gross Domestic Product (GDP). To be remarked is that the share of Asia includes Japan.

international economic order" championed in the 1970s by the Group of 77, the UN lobby of the developing countries. After the failure of the 1980 special session of the General Assembly to launch the "global dialogue," contact between the economies of North and South, instead of becoming organized in view of mutual accommodation, became, in the words of Willy Brandt, then chairman of the North-South Commission, a dialogue of the deaf. In the 1980s, most attempts at a global organization of the world economy were dismissed as being state interventionist and possibly dictatorial. The evident failure of centralized economic planning in 1989 reinforced this posture. But meanwhile financial flows became rapidly informatized and, in consequence, globalized. And the globalized financial system became ever more unstable and prone to crisis.

By now, the lack of a coordinated approach is making itself felt, despite the persistent mistrust of international economic governance in free-market-oriented states. It is becoming evident that in order to stimulate global economic growth, and even to prevent periodic depression and breakdown, better coordination is needed in attempts at public-interest interventions in the international financial system. The issue is acute for poor countries, which need a more generous and reliable stream of transnational direct investment. But it is also felt in the affluent countries. They are exposed to volatile financial markets and critical fluctuations in the value of their currencies.

While public policy remains an important element in world affairs, it is also true that today national governments are no longer the sole actors on the international scene. The more than 190 national governments and roughly 10,000 international or intergovernmental organizations are joined by a thousand or more business corporations as major global players. The leading domestic industries of the 1950s have grown into the multinationals of the 1960s and seventies and the transnationals and globals of the eighties and nineties.

GLOBALIZATION IN BUSINESS

The full extent of globalization in business is seldom recognized. The confluence of production, commerce, technologies of control and information, and the changing political scene provided major industrial and financial enterprises with the opportunity and the means to span the world. They soon did. The process was pioneered by U.S. manufacturing companies in the postwar years. Prompted by the low cost of labor, they extended beyond the continental United States to Latin America, Europe, and the Far East.

Worldwide flows of information became major drivers of the corporate globalization process. Since information can spread rapidly from company to company, it had become more difficult to build competitive advantage through the commercialization of inventions. When the information base of innovation became globally accessible, imitation quickly led to the dissipation of profits in new projects. As a result, firms turned to new forms of growth and profitability. On the one hand, they moved further downstream into consumer and service areas, and on the other they expanded horizontally, through mergers and acquisitions. This created significant growth in the size, scope, and geographic span of the leading enterprises. Government deregulation and tax benefits promoted the expansion process; tax rate differentials across countries prompted companies to invest, or establish an actual presence, in a variety of national markets.

The creation of multinational companies constituted one stage in the globalization of the private sector; the next stage was the emergence of transnational, genuinely global corporations. By the late 1980s no country was holding a monopoly on technology, capital, talent, and innovation, and in the continued search for profit and growth multinational companies went global. Today, the leading enterprises are global in organization and production as well as in products. Divisional headquarters are internationally decentralized—even traditionally

U.S.-centered IBM moved one of its product headquarters overseas.

Globalized companies are making breakthroughs in the laboratories of one country, place shares with investors from others, and put the nationals of still others on a fast track to the top. Their products now include components from pretty well all over the world. The 1989 Volkswagen Rabbit, for example, though assembled in Germany, has components manufactured in France, England, Austria, Switzerland, Holland, Italy, Sweden, the United States, Canada, Spain, Portugal, Hungary, Brazil, Mexico, Japan, and South Africa. Specific products and services also come from Belgium, Denmark, Finland, Norway, and Luxemburg. Siemens, an electronics giant with eighty-seven business units in 131 countries, admitted that it cannot any longer trace in detail the origin of the components that go into its 55,000 products. As supplier-producer-marketing cooperation complexifies and intensifies—through acquisitions, mergers, as well as strategic alliances—many a specialized "niche player" turns into a diversified and geographically extended "global player."

The globalization of the Fortune 500 companies—long headed by the automakers, an electronics giant, and the "seven sisters" oil companies—was accompanied by the globalization of trade and service companies, and paralleled by financial markets operating "round the clock and round the world." The exchange market has become the most global of all business sectors, with worldwide rates, instantaneous electronic banking and arbitrage, and a daily turnover estimated in excess of $700 billion.

The Power of Global Corporations. Global companies command an unprecedented share of wealth in the world economy. In 1976, the revenues of the 200 largest companies equaled about one-sixth of the world's gross domestic product; by 1988, the same share in world GDP was concentrated in the 100 largest companies. The "Fortune Top 5" (GM, Ford,

Exxon, Shell, and IBM) had more than 3 percent of the GDP of the 120 countries reporting to the World Bank (that is, total revenues of $431 billion, compared with a world GDP of roughly $14,000 billion). In terms of wealth, global companies have overtaken numerous national economies. By 1988, the combined revenue of the three largest manufacturing companies (GM, Ford, and Exxon) surpassed Brazil's gross domestic product, and the revenues of the seventeen largest industrial manufacturing companies (about $922 billion) equaled the revenues of fifty of the world's poorest countries, the home of 65 percent of the world population.

Today's business companies are decisive actors in the contemporary world. Although even global corporations seldom number more than 100,000 employees, while national governments claim to represent many millions of people, particular businesses often control crucial sectors of the economy with as much strategic impact as national governments. By creating employment, corporations influence the distribution of wealth and create social stability. By bringing value-added products and services to the marketplace, they raise the material standard of living. Through investments they transform the fabric of society, influencing lifestyles, employment opportunities, and the balance between urban and rural environments. And if they adopt irresponsible attitudes toward society and the ecology, industrial corporations degenerate local environments, deprive large segments of the population of work, and condemn entire economies to poverty and underdevelopment.

The decisions of global corporations affect not only the businesses and markets in which they function, but also the lives and environments of the people in whose communities they operate. The lives of traditional populations in India, and the economies of Communist-dominated regions in Eastern Europe were suddenly and dramatically transformed when global companies such as Dow, General Electric, and Siemens bought local plants and invested in new production and distribution facilities.

The grand transition has changed our world from A to Z. The private as well as the public sector became immersed in a continually growing stream of globe-circling information. In the attempt to access the stream and make use of it, both national governments and business corporations have been reaching beyond traditional boundaries, pulling themselves by their bootstraps toward globality. Business corporations and networks have reached the global dimension already. Unlike governments, they were not hampered by constitutional and pragmatic ties to national constituencies and interests.

Informatization and globalization are basic drivers of the grand transition. If they continue to drive social and economic processes in the future, humanity will be impelled into a globally integrated, interdependent yet cooperative world. But whether it will actually reach this condition is by no means certain.

As we shall see next, the path of the grand transition is filled with shocks and surprises.

2

Where We Are Headed: The Shock Waves

FOUR WAVES DOWN, ONE TO GO

Since the beginning of this century, the human community has undergone a series of four shock waves powerful enough to redraw the social, economic, and political map of the world. The first shock was the Bolshevik coup engineered by Lenin; the second the rise of Hitler and the national socialists to power. The third shock wave catalyzed the liberation of Europe's colonies, while the fourth liberalized the Communist-dominated countries and marked the downfall of the system created by Lenin.

A fifth wave, if not better managed than these, could jeopardize the entire grand transition.

The First Wave: Communism. The events seventy-seven years ago that led to the transformation of czarist Russia into the Communist party–led Soviet Union had deep roots. Failure to modernize its social, economic, and political structures during the nineteenth century left the Russian czarist regime unstable and rigid; the 1904 war with Japan had led to a nearly successful revolt that took place in 1905. Attempts to accelerate reforms were frustrated by conservative political forces, while economic growth, industrialization, and social unrest created increased tensions. The result was a government that alienated its middle-class supporters and drove the peasants and workers toward ever more violence. By 1914 the nation was greatly divided; the outbreak of the war could only delay a full-scale revolution by temporarily redirecting crucial social and political energies. The traumatic events of World War I sealed its fate.

Nicholas II's inability to govern created a deep crisis, aggravated by humiliating defeats suffered at the hand of the Germans. Corruption in the state bureaucracy led to a desperate shortage of arms, as well as of such basic necessities as clothing and food. In February 1917 food riots had broken out, the economic and political system had collapsed, and the Romanov dynasty had been toppled.

The speed and thoroughness of the collapse of the czarist regime surprised even those who had devoted their lives to its revolutionary overthrow. Even more surprising was the revolution's outcome. Stalin and the Petrograd leadership had supported the provisional government for months; *Pravda* actually printed articles opposing the plans of Lenin and Trotsky to "telescope" the stages of the transformation by seizing power in November. At the critical moment, Lenin despaired of success, and only Trotsky was able to dissuade him from fleeing to Finland. But then Allied demands that Russia honor its treaties and continue fighting the war made it impossible for the provisional government to solve the mounting social and economic problems. Internal class antagonisms, exacerbated by oppressive policies and poor military performance, were brought to the boiling point by gross corruption. The country was ripe for change.

Even though the Bolsheviks were a relatively minor movement, they could rise up in the chaos of the power vacuum: Lenin had succeeded in stepping in at the crucial moment. His "April Theses" proved increasingly attractive in the deepening crisis. The slogan "Bread, Land, and Peace" promised to meet the most basic needs of the peasants, and it maneuvered the Bolsheviks into position as leaders of the urban workers as well; their prewar violence had been only briefly contained by patriotic appeals. By November 1917 increasing radicalism among urban groups, soldiers, and peasants tipped the scales, together with Lenin's political and oratorical skills, Trotsky's genius for military organization, and the efficiency of the revitalized Bolshevik apparatus.

In the aftermath of the 1917 Revolution the Bolsheviks, led by Lenin, established the Soviet system with the Communist Party as its vanguard. The Communist wave rolled over White Russia, the Ukraine, the Baltic States, and into various southern and Asian regions, all of which became Soviet Socialist Republics. The successful conclusion of World War II levered the Soviet Union into superpower status, with the Communist wave rolling into Eastern Europe and spreading to China, Cuba, Vietnam, Korea, and other parts of Asia as well as to Africa. It was weakened subsequently by economic, ideologic, and political problems; and when the final dissolution of the Soviet Empire came in 1991, it created another shock wave that spread all over the world.

The Second Wave: Fascism. The second wave began with the rise of Fascism in Italy and shifted into global gear when Germany transformed from the Weimar Republic into the National Socialist Third Reich. The events that launched this wave were less telescoped in time than the events in Russia, but they were similar in many respects and not any the less dramatic.

The name "fascism" was first attached to a political movement in Italy by Benito Mussolini in 1919. (The term itself derives from the Latin *fasces*: bundles of elm or birch rods from which the head of an ax projected, fastened together by a red strap. Originally symbolizing the power of kings to scourge and to decapitate, fasces were borne before Roman emperors, praetors, and magistrates as a symbol of their authority.) Mussolini's movement extolled the power of the state and subordinated all other considerations to it. It gained power in the period of disillusionment that beset Italy after the lost war of 1914–1918. On March 23, 1919, Mussolini founded the Fasci di Combattimento, a radical group that had no definite program but preached the expropriation of land, the mines, and all means of transportation. Mussolini and his determined squads of young followers appeared to the frightened upper classes of the time as possible guarantors of security. With the agreement of the army, Mussolini set about what he called "restoring order" and conquering, in the name of Italian youth, the "tottering parliamentism of senile and undecided liberals."

Emboldened by lack of resistance by army, police, and government, in 1921 the Italian Fascists formed themselves into the National Fascist Party. On October 28, 1922, they staged the famous march on Rome, and though in parliament they were outnumbered by ten to one, the next day the king invited Mussolini to form a new government. Mussolini did so, with the result that within a few years all traces of parliamentarism were gone, all other political parties were outlawed, and all civil liberties and constitutional guarantees were suppressed. The Fascists established a totalitarian order in which the nation was completely identified with the Fascist Party, and the Fascist Party was completely identified with Mussolini.

Fascism, which in the 1920s was confined to Italy, became a worldwide movement in the 1930s. Its propaganda machinery was active not only in Europe but throughout the Western Hemisphere. Fascists claimed the inevitable breakdown of parliamentary democracy and their own equally inevitable upsurge as "the wave of the future." By the end of the 1930s Fascist movements swept Latin America and even Asia, where Japan became a major Fascist power. But the crucial step was the rise of Hitler's Nazi Party in Germany. It borrowed and adapted many of the ideas and slogans of Mussolini's Fascists and, from 1936 on, when Germany and Italy entered into a wide range of political, economic, and military accords, dominated and transformed the worldwide Fascist movement.

The rise of the National Socialists in Germany was due to circumstances that had much in common with the rise of the Fascists in Italy and the Bolsheviks in Russia. Having entered

World War I as the strongest power on the Continent, Germany's defeat created a major trauma for its people. Scapegoats had to be found to explain how a magnificent army, countless acts of personal courage, and extensive national sacrifices culminated in a humiliating loss of territory, sovereignty, and foreign colonies, and the bankruptcy of a powerful economy backed by great industrial might. Mutual recriminations between conservatives and socialists, republicans and monarchists, and between various segments of society led to growing internal fragmentation. The rapid introduction of industrial technology into Wilhelmian Germany already had destabilized its traditional institutions and created deep and widespread alienation. Compounded by defeat and the humiliation of the Treaty of Versailles, social institutions collapsed and revolts became a frequent occurrence. Street fighting was rampant, "political" murders became common, and civil war seemed imminent.

War debts, the penury inflicted by the Versailles Treaty, foreign interventions, and a devastating inflation kept the German economy in crisis. When an Austrian bank broke the crucial cycle of payments, unemployment reached all-time highs. In these turbulent times, Adolf Hitler rose meteorically to power.

In normal times this Austrian corporal, who had failed as an architect and whose accent was so alien that Prussians ridiculed it, would have been an unlikely choice in the sophisticated Weimar Republic. His party platform was so contradictory that he thought best to promise not to implement it, and his attempt to seize power during the 1923 financial crisis had ended in imprisonment. Yet in the wake of the Reichstag fire—of which the causes remain obscure to this day—Hitler managed to use the power of propaganda to make himself and his already powerful Nazi Party practically invincible.

Extolling the virtues of the Aryan race and the destiny of the German state, and promising to revenge lost wealth and prestige by bringing Germany to the pinnacle of world power,

Hitler's atavistic policies and personality overcame the frustration and alienation of the postwar decade and rallied German society to a new cause, however inhuman and violent. Driven by the powerful German war machine, the Fascist wave rolled over most of continental Europe, North Africa, and into Russia. Except for a series of desperate courageous acts, it would have rolled over England as well, and if the United States had not come into the picture (and if Hitler had not failed to win the race to create the atomic bomb), it would have engulfed the whole of the civilized world.

The Third Wave: Decolonization. Both the first and the second shock waves of the twentieth century were spin-offs of World War I; the second wave led directly to World War II. But the third wave was a spin-off of the way World War II ended. The victory of the Allied powers in 1945 led to the division of Europe at Yalta, and to the strengthening of the Communist system created by the first wave. It also led to a widespread debate among the victorious powers regarding the propriety and feasibility of maintaining overseas colonies. These colonies were first acquired by European states in the sixteenth century, in a mercantile drive to accumulate reserves of precious metals and acquire a balance of trade that would reflect, and indeed be a measure of, their prestige and power. But in the middle of the twentieth century, in the aftermath of the cataclysm of World War II, the perceived value of the colonies had paled considerably. Germany and Italy had lost their overseas colonies, and, prompted by the Versailles Treaty of 1919, the victorious powers of Europe decided to give up theirs.

    Decolonization had a noble motivation: It was to allow entry to all the peoples of the world into a system that, while in practice dominated by the Allied powers, would observe the democratic principle of equality among sovereign states. In 1945 similar motivations inspired a new try at creating a world organization to replace the defunct League of Nations; and the newly liberated states were encouraged to join the fledgling United Nations.

The wave of decolonization succeeded in bringing traditional peoples into the orbit of the modern world. But decolonization did not entirely achieve its noble objective: It granted de jure independence to the former colonies but left them in a condition of de facto economic dependence. European powers were reluctant to surrender their privileged access to the natural resources and growing markets of their former possessions. Information, energy, trade, and technology continued to flow along channels dominated by the industrialized countries, making for a form of colonialism that was economic even if it was no longer political. As to the newly liberated countries themselves, they were caught in a disorienting and disrupting vortex that polarized social classes and led to new forms of injustice and inequity.

Much like the unprepared nations of Latin America, the freshly decolonized countries became torn by deep internal divisions. Their plight was worsened by the population explosion triggered by the introduction of more hygienic conditions and new medical practices. These led to a rapid reduction of mortality rates without at the same time reducing the traditionally high fertility rates.

Lacking access to technologies, information, and capital, inexperienced, and sometimes power-hungry, the leaders of the world's formally sovereign but in fact highly dependent countries were unable to bring about lasting socioeconomic progress. As the small modernized sector detached itself from the still traditional main body of society, the economy became polarized and the social fabric was rent asunder. A vicious cycle developed in which poverty fueled population growth, and population growth dissipated the benefits of social and economic progress and exacerbated poverty.

In subsequent years, governments and major corporations aggravated the plight of the decolonized countries by focusing aid and investment in the comparatively few states that managed to make real economic progress. To this day, ten countries (Argentina, Brazil, China, Colombia, Egypt, Hong Kong, Malaysia, Mexico, Singapore, and Thailand) are receiving as much as 75 percent of the direct investment flowing toward the developing countries as a whole. In the well over 100 countries that make up the rest of that group, economic development never had a chance to take off.

The Fourth Wave: Glasnost. The next major twentieth-century shock wave began in 1985 with Mikhail Gorbachev's policy of glasnost. Glasnost opened the second world of Socialist countries to world markets, much as decolonization had opened the third world. The result was just as unexpected and far more sudden. As soon as the people of Eastern Europe were freed from the constraints of autocratic one-party rule, they organized themselves and rebelled. Hungary, Poland, and the former East Germany led the way; Czechoslovakia, the Baltic States, and even Romania, Bulgaria, and Albania soon followed. The Soviet Union was not far behind.

Glasnost was to produce perestroika—"openness" was to lead to "restructuring." But perestroika encountered major obstacles: As a planned process, it enlarged only slightly the scope for private and entrepreneurial initiative and reduced somewhat the state bureaucracy. The frustration triggered by its failure brought down the leadership that set it into motion. By 1991 the government headed by Gorbachev was facing a near total breakdown of the economy, a collapse of party and state authority in the republics, hostility between Moscow and the non-Russian republics, with secession movements in the Baltic and Islamic republics, the emergence of a Solidarity-like workers' movement in the industrial regions, and public unrest caused by chronic food shortages and inflation. It also faced growing resistance by the reformers, who believed that the leadership did not go far enough, and by the hard-liners, who thought that it went too far. It took ongoing polemics with the former and an almost fatal coup by the latter to bring perestroika into real motion. By then the process turned into a full-scale uprooting and transformation of the Socialist system, rather than its adaptive restructuring.

Glasnost reached an unforeseen apex in the summer of 1991, when the Communist Party of the Soviet Union was outlawed and Lenin was removed as prophet and hero of the Soviet people. A few months later a still more surprising outcome materialized: The Soviet Union itself came to an end, and Gorbachev fell from power. In place of the monolithic Communist empire a plethora of ethnic and political fragments came on the East European scene. Where political independence was poorly aligned with the ethnic origins and solidarity of the people (as in the former Yugoslavia), the fragmented states fragmented still further, causing violence reminiscent of the worst excesses of the Nazi regime.

When the Kremlin's atheistic world empire fell, the absence of a common enemy allowed self-assertion, rivalry, and animosity to arise among religious groups. It created outbreaks of fundamentalism in the Middle East and fueled religious strife on the Indian subcontinent as well as in parts of Central and South America. Strife among the newly liberated ethnic groups is still rampant. In addition to Bosnia-Herzegovina and the Serb-Croat-Muslim conflict, there are smoldering hot spots in Transylvania and Slovakia, given their repressed and no longer Red army–constrained Hungarian minorities. There are hundreds of thousands of Poles in similar situations, inhabiting regions bordering on their country, and millions of Russians spread throughout the now independent—and intensely resentful—territories of the Commonwealth of Independent States. Similarly threatening ethnic minority problems beset large regions of Asia, Africa, and the Americas, though they are not a direct legacy of glasnost.

A Fifth Wave? As this historical retrospective has shown, there have been at least four major shock waves stressing the world community in the twentieth century. But, though four waves are behind us, a fifth wave may be ahead of us. Indeed, the possibility that such a wave is on the horizon is extremely high. The late twentieth-century world is overpopulated, overpolluted, overarmed, and extremely energy- and resource-hungry. It is also increasingly polarized, with a small minority of well-off industrialized countries surrounded by a rising sea of poor, underdeveloped states. These conditions are not unrelated to the outcome of the previous waves: They are in some ways their unintended consequences.

The nature of the social, economic, ecologic, and political processes that now lead the world community from the four waves in the past to a fifth wave that approaches can be reconstructed. The ongoing informatization and globalization of society created tensions that were aggravated by the availability of weapons of massive and impersonal destruction. Uncontrolled tensions led to two world wars, the bitter experience of which created an ideology of democracy and equality that produced the third world. Then, the unequitable flow of information and technologies to the people of that world created further problems. Among other things it dropped the death rate without dropping the birth rate: It thus created a population explosion. This reduced the chances of economic growth and reinforced poverty. Ever more people witnessed the collapse of the "revolution of rising expectations" into a vicious cycle in which having many children sustained poverty, and poverty sustained a perceived need for many children.

The international community, rent by economic and social imbalance and global and local antagonisms, armed itself to the teeth, making the worst of its perilous situation. It let hardly a day go by without fighting a war. And when it was not fighting wars, it kept itself in a state of utmost preparedness for them. This made for overmilitarization in a world in large part overpopulated and underdeveloped.

In the economically advanced countries, growing competition for wealth and power created an unreflective scramble for the resources required to feed and operate the sacrosanct instruments of wealth and power: the new technologies of production, consumption, and communication. At the same time, producing mountains of by-products and waste, giant industries and urban complexes overexploited their resource base and overloaded the regenerative cycles of their life-support systems. The results were the impairment of long-established balances in the biosphere and in the atmosphere, creating changed weather patterns, toxins in soil, air, and water; and recurrent shortages of food and energy.

THE FIFTH WAVE: GLOBAL STRESS

Problems of population, poverty, militarization, waste and environmental degradation, climate change, and food and energy shortages are the principal causes of intensifying stress in the global system. They are the factors that trigger the fifth wave and merit a more detailed look.

Population. Population is one of the most basic, and certainly the most controversial, of all global stress factors. Some see it as the crux of all world problems, while others consider it but a spin-off of more fundamental issues.

The population problem is a modern-age phenomenon. Before the Neolithic revolution, there were perhaps 4 million humans on this planet, nomadic hunters-gatherers for the most part. The agricultural revolution boosted the population by providing excess food; by the time of Jesus some 175 million humans inhabited the planet. It then took fully fourteen centuries to double the population to 350 million. The first billion was reached in 1810; the second in 1930, and the third in 1960. Since then another two and a half billion have been added, and in the present decade one more billion will be added again.

This increase is geometrical, progressing as the ratio of 1 to 2, to 4, to 8, etc. On the other hand, food and other life necessities may only increase in an arithmetical fashion, as 1 to 2, to 3, to 4, and so on. This, said Thomas Malthus in his 1798 *Essay on the Principle of Population,* is bound to end in catastrophe. "The power of population," he said, "is indefinitely greater than the power in the earth to produce subsistence for man."

Those who in recent times revived the population problem tended to take their clue from Malthus. Ecologist Paul Ehrlich, for example, predicted in his 1967 *The Population Bomb* that unless plague or thermonuclear war kills off large masses first, there will be vast famines, with hundreds of millions starving to death between 1970 and 1985. Though he later revised the time estimate, he continued to maintain that unless determined measures were taken, mass starvation, epidemics, and a reversion to the Dark Ages would be the consequence.

Different views are held of the population problem in different parts of the world.

The developed world view. Although few people condone the coercive approach to the problem advocated by desperate Malthusians, many and perhaps most people in the developed

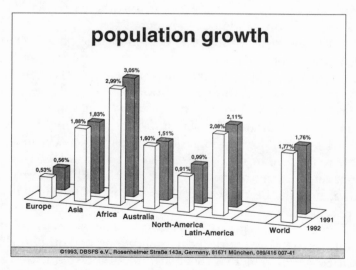

The growth rate of the world population, by continent (1991–92).

world see the population explosion as the number-one world problem—a problem predominantly of the developing countries. Already in 1983, three-fourths of the world's peoples lived in the developing countries and only one-fourth in the rest. In the year 2000, 79 percent of the global population is expected to be in the third world, and in the year 2020, 83 percent. The developing countries need to take determined steps to halt this population explosion.

The socialist and third world view. Socialists and third-world leaders espouse a different view: They see the population issue as a spin-off of the unjust distribution of wealth in the international system. Population growth is not the cause of the problem, they say, it is but a symptom of deeper causes, such as unequal landholding, cash cropping, and the vicious cycle of debts paid off at the cost of more loans and greater debt. In their view economic development is the best contraceptive: As standards of living improve, population growth will slow and eventually come to a halt. The rich countries must take determined steps to ensure a more equitable distribution of global wealth.

Regardless of the assignation of blame, the fact is that third-world economic development can seldom get off the ground, since modest increases in economic wealth are swallowed by greater increases in human numbers. Giving priority to health, education, and women's rights proves to be essential to lowering fertility and to breaking the vicious cycle of poverty breeding children and children breeding more poverty. But birth control runs into opposition by groups as varied as Moslem fundamentalists, Roman Catholics, some feminists, and many developing-country intellectuals. The insistence of third-world governments that the number-one problem is economic injustice, coupled with the load placed on resources and the environment by the industrialized countries, has brought action on population effectively to a halt. Not even at the 1992 Rio "Earth Summit" could the problem be addressed without taking out all mention of contraceptives and inserting euphemisms for family planning.

As a result, despite a notable decrease in fertility rates in a few parts of the world, the population explosion is continuing. The population of Africa, the poorest continent, is expected to triple in the forty-five years between 1980 and 2025, growing from 500 million to a billion and a half; and the population of Bangladesh could double in the next thirty-five years, going from 110 to 220 million. Similar growth rates are projected for many parts of Asia, Africa, and Latin America. On the global level, the upward-revised UN demographic projections show that three people are added to the world population every second. The daily increment is more than a quarter of a million human beings, equivalent to the population of a large town; the annual figure is 97 million, more than the population of reunified Germany. At least for the rest of this decade, the population of the globe will continue to inflate at this rate, reaching 6 billion by the year 2000.

A large segment of the world population is just entering the age of fertility. At the beginning of the twenty-first century fully one-third of the human population is expected to be teenagers, living predominantly in Asia, Africa, and Latin America. But most teenage women in developing countries are neither sufficiently informed nor sufficiently emancipated to have only those children they want to have. According to the World Health Organization, there are about 100 million acts of sexual intercourse every day, and 910,000 of them result in conception. If this process were to continue, the world population would grow to 12 to 14 billion before stabilizing sometime in the middle of the twenty-first century. And by that time far more than half the world's population would be Asian, and almost a fifth African.

The age distribution of the population poses further problems. While the developing world will grow in absolute numbers, the industrialized world will grow only in age. People aged sixty and over currently comprise 12.5 percent of the population in North America, 14 percent in Western Europe, and 10.5 percent in Eastern Europe. But, according to the projections of the Population Program of the International Institute of Applied Systems Analysis (IIASA), by the year 2050 the aged population of Europe and North America may comprise as much as 44 percent of the total. At the same time, the proportion of young people (under the age of twenty), which is now 21.4 percent in North America, 18.6 percent in Western Europe, and 22.6 percent in Eastern Europe, will drop as soon as the present baby-boom generation has its own share of babies. This means that the total population of North America and Europe (including the newly independent Soviet republics), now just over 1 billion, will increase marginally until about 2010, and then drop to about 771 million by the year 2050. By that time it will be less than 10 percent of the world total.

The population picture is not complete, however, until we take the local concentration of population groups into account. In 1950, the world population was still predominantly rural, and thus relatively dispersed. Only about 600 million people lived in cities, while today more than 2 billion do. And by the year 2020 two-thirds of the world population may be residents of urban areas, some of them of staggering dimensions.

The number of third-world cities with more than 4 million people is predicted to grow to sixty at the turn of the century, and 135 by 2025. The population of cities grows much faster than the overall population; and the population of third-world cities grows fastest of all. According to the UN's demographic

1992
Total: 5.26 billion

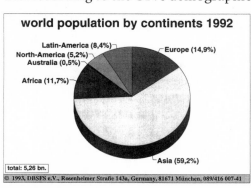

world population by continents 1992

Latin-America (8,4%)
North-America (5,2%)
Australia (0,5%)
Africa (11,7%)
Europe (14,9%)
Asia (59,2%)

total: 5,26 bn.

© 1993, DBSFS e.V., Rosenheimer Straße 143a, Germany, 81671 München, 089/416 007-41

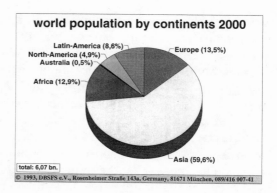

2000
Total: 6.07 billion

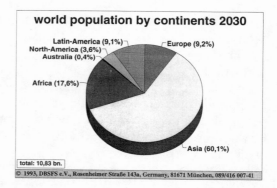

2030
Total: 10.83 billion

projections, by the turn of the century seventeen of the twenty
emerging urban megacomplexes with more than 11 million in-
habitants will be in the developing countries. At that time
77 percent of Latin America, 41 percent of Africa, and 35 percent of Asia will be urbanized. Mexico City has already overtaken all urban agglomerations in sheer population size, and is
closely followed by São Paulo, Lagos, Bombay, and Seoul.

Third world cities cannot provide work for such population increments: According to rather conservative UN estimates, the 700 million unemployed—or only partially and
occasionally employed—people of today's developing world

will rise toward the one-billion mark by the turn of the century, with the vast majority in the rapidly growing urban agglomerations.

Then we must add the factor of migration: the movement of vast populations. The shock waves of this century produced major waves of migrants on continent after continent. There are now at least 15 million people permanently without a country; about 12.5 million roam sub-Saharan Africa alone. There are more than 70 million men and women (though in the majority men) who work far from their home countries, mainly in Europe and North America. These "guest workers" are but the privileged tip of an iceberg of destitute and increasingly desperate people. Mass migrations have become part of the contemporary demographic world picture: Since the beginning of this century an estimated 250 million people have left their native lands in search of a better life.

Each year an estimated 1 million illegal immigrants cross the border from Mexico to the United States; at least 15 million migrants, both legal and illegal, may cross during the 1990s and another 30 million could arrive by the year 2020. As the migrant stream swells, by 2030 three minorities—Hispanic, Black, and Asian—will make up the majority of the U.S. population. Similar multicultural shifts are in store in Europe. A small but steadily increasing stream of migrants is moving from North Africa to Spain and beyond, made up of destitute and desperate individuals who pay their last penny for a perilous boat ride across the Strait of Gibraltar, often completed by swimming the last few hundred meters. Police found dozens of bodies on Spanish beaches, and in the first nine months of 1992 alone picked up more than 1,500 illegal immigrants.

Poverty. The causes of global stress—the fifth wave likely to descend on humanity in this century—are not limited to population. The side effects of poverty, of the unreflected use of unadapted technologies, and even of affluence, play an equally important role. Thus, to understand the causes and possible remedies of the shock wave now on the horizon, we should also look at such factors as poverty and waste, and their manifold consequences.

According to conservative World Bank estimates, the 500 million people who in the early 1980s lived under the threshold of absolute poverty—that is, on less than $370 a year—grew to 1 billion by 1990. One and a half billion people do not have access even to the most rudimentary health services, while the number of those without safe drinking water is about 2 billion.

There is a corresponding increase in the number of critically impoverished countries. In 1964 there were twenty-four states on the UN's list of LDCs (least developed countries); in 1980 there were thirty-one. But by 1990 there were forty-two—a 75 percent increase in twenty years. In 1970 there was only one country (Chad) that experienced a continuing decline in GNP per capita; in 1980 there were thirty-five such countries. And by 1990 no less than ninety countries were losing the race between population and development.

The richest 20 percent of the world population has not ten times or even twenty times the income of the poorest 20 percent, but 150 times. But there is poverty also in the rich countries. In the United States currently 14 percent of the people live at or below the poverty level. At the same time, the family income of the wealthiest 5 percent of the population has risen by 23 percent in the last decade and has now reached 22.5 times the income of those at the poverty level. And the income of the poorest 25 percent of Americans has declined by an estimated 6 percent.

Because of spreading poverty, many parts of the world experience falling life expectancy, rising infant mortality, and recurrent famine. In twenty-one out of thirty-five low-income developing countries, the overall daily calorie supply per capita was lower in 1985 than it was in 1965; almost half of the 115 developing countries experienced falling per capita staple food consumption in the last ten years. Today there are

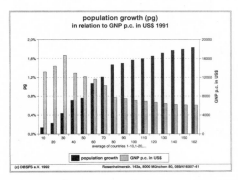

Population growth rate in relation to per capita GNP (average values of groups of ten countries, in a total of 162 countries).

more than 100 million Africans with acute food deficiency, 60 million are on the edge of starvation, and nobody knows how many millions die of AIDS. In South Asia some 200 million people live permanently in the shadow of famine and disease.

The economic problems of the poor countries are only partly due to mismanagement and an unequal distribution of the wealth. In part they have structural causes, including the loan policies espoused by major lenders. In the expectation that loan capital would trigger rapid economic growth and produce quick returns, commercial banks and public financial institutions pumped large amounts of capital into developing regions throughout the 1960s and seventies. In the 1980s, however, the international loan departments of the big banks changed from corporate stars to emergency wards.

Attempts to recover principal and interest on outstanding loans have cemented the economic plight of many developing countries: They have been exposed to what the International Monetary Fund calls "discipline" in their economic policies. Often, this has put a halt to development altogether.

Since 1983, the international flow of capital has reversed: According to the World Bank, it now moves from the "South" to the "North"—that is, from the poor to the rich countries.

The reverse flow (calculated by deducting capital repayments and interest payments from monies received as new loans) grew from $1.4 billion in 1983 to $40 billion in 1988. It is currently estimated in excess of $60 billion.

Such inflow of capital that still exists is highly concentrated. The UN's *1991 World Investment Report* noted that of the total flow of investment capital in 1990, $163 billion went to the developed economies and just $30 billion to the group that is officially defined as the developing countries. In fact, three-fourths of this already small slice went to ten countries, of which at least half (Singapore, Hong Kong, Brazil, Mexico, and Argentina) are quite industrialized. The forty-two least developed countries had to content themselves with only 0.7 percent of the private capital invested in the third world as a whole.

The private sector is not bailing out the world's poorest peoples and economies, and the public sector, whose job it would be to tackle the issues that threaten the common good, is only marginally helpful. While the governments of the industrialized world do provide aid for development, the dimensions of aid are linked to considerations that have little to do with the welfare of the recipients.

For example, in South Asia, where fully one-half of the world's poorest people live, in 1992 each person received around $5 in aid, while in the Middle East, where the average income is three times higher, he or she obtained about $55. Countries that are spending great sums of money on weapons are often provided twice as much foreign aid per person than other countries. And the amount of aid specifically earmarked for projects designed to meet the woes of the poor people seldom exceeds one-third of the aid package, while the combined aid spent on meeting basic needs—such as primary health care, safe drinking water, nutrition, sanitation, education, and family planning—comes only to about 7 percent of country-to-country aid flows and 10 percent of aid channeled through the UN or other multilateral agencies.

Militarization. The causes of global stress are demographic and ecological, yet governments also spend far more on their own military establishments than on remedying economic, social, and environmental woes—their own, not to mention that of others. As recently as 1990, 142 states maintained standing armies. Today the number of sovereign states is inflated by the secession of the republics of the former Soviet Union and Yugoslavia. Since most of the new states decided to create their own armed forces, the number of national armies has been growing apace.

Even though the cold war has wound down, the world's military establishments still employ more than 2 percent of the global labor force and cost an estimated $1,000 billion a year. Until recently the largest spenders were the two superpowers. However, the Russian Republic that succeeded the U.S.S.R. as the major military entity of the region is scarcely in a position to foot the bill for continuing the arms race. The 1992 Bush-Yeltsin strategic-arms-reduction accord allowed Russia heavy cuts in military spending, while the Clinton administration insists on a phased reduction of military spending in the United States.

There is no corresponding reduction in the third world. Almost one-third of current world armaments spending is by developing-country governments. As the great powers are cutting back on their own military budgets, this proportion will no doubt increase in coming years.

Waste and Pollution. Despite a growing awareness of resource and environmental problems, and notwithstanding gains in energy efficiency and the adoption of recycling practices, the world's affluent populations remain relatively wasteful of natural resources. This is a major cause of the global stress syndrome. It is estimated that a child coming into the world in the United States and living for eighty-two years will consume a total of 56 million gallons of water, 21,000 tons of gasoline, 100,000 pounds of steel, the wood of 1,000 trees—and will produce nearly sixty tons of municipal waste. Not surprisingly, between 1970 and 1988 the volume of municipal solid waste (landfilled or incinerated) rose by 37 percent. A quarter of this waste is made up of discarded food and garden waste; the biggest share among throwaway items is that of disposable diapers. American hospitals generate on the average thirteen pounds of waste per day for each bed, the bulk of which is made up of disposable sheets and dressings.

Such levels of resource consumption and waste generation, even if dictated by considerations of immediate local benefit, cannot continue for long. Not only would stocks of nonrenewable resources run out; even space would run out on which to dump the wastes. In the United States, the Environmental Protection Agency estimates that 80 percent of existing landfills will close by the first few years of the next century, with some states on the East Coast running out of landfill capacity by the mid-nineties. Holland has already exhausted its landfill sites, and Japan will run out by about 2005. Because of the shortage of domestic dumping grounds, more and more industrialized countries have been exporting their wastes to the third world. This practice, however, cannot be set forth indefinitely: Developing country governments are increasingly objecting to being used as dumping grounds. And Russia and the rest of Eastern Europe, formerly a willing and convenient dumping area for Western Europe, has closed down since 1990.

The poor countries not only object to being dumping grounds for the rich; they want to become rich themselves, or at least more prosperous than at present. This would mean a significant rise in resource consumption and waste generation the world over. But the consumption and waste levels presently attained by the industrialized countries could never be duplicated in the developing ones. Our planet would be depleted and overpolluted within a generation.

Poverty, however, can wreak as much havoc as affluence. In the poorest parts of the world, topsoils and forests are vanishing not because of excessive doses of chemical fertilizers and pesticides, but because of overgrazing and overcropping, the persistence of slash-and-burn agriculture, and reliance on fire-wood and dung for heating and cooking. Countries such as Poland produce five times more sulfur dioxide and solid waste per unit of GNP than Western Europe. The end result of such practices is the same, whether they are due to affluence or to penury: environmental degradation, soil erosion, acid rain, and the warming of the global atmosphere.

Whenever and wherever fossil fuels are burnt, the elements carbon, sulfur, and nitrogen oxidize in the atmosphere. As each of these elements combines with oxygen, carbon dioxide, sulfur dioxide, and various nitrogen oxides are produced. Of these gases, carbon dioxide (CO_2) is the most dangerous: Large quantities of it could depress the ability of the biosphere to maintain its regenerative cycles and sustain life. It is of concern, therefore, that currently some 7 billion tons of carbon dioxide are pumped into the atmosphere each year, 45 percent of it by the twenty-four member states of the OECD (Organization for Economic Cooperation and Development), the club of industrialized countries. The OECD's econometric model known as GREEN showed that in order to stabilize CO_2 emissions at the 1990 levels, its member states would need to cut "business as usual" emissions by 44 percent between now and the year 2050. These drastic reductions would entail nearly unbearable economic costs—and they would not be of much use by themselves. If countries such as China and India continued to increase their carbon emissions by the current annual average of 3.7 and 3.9 percent, worldwide emissions would be only 11 percent less than at the "business as usual" rates.

Independent estimates confirm that holding constant the amount of CO_2 already in the atmosphere at the current levels calls for a reduction of at least 50 percent in worldwide fossil-fuel use. If the current CO_2 levels are to be actually reduced, world energy consumption would have to be cut back by at least 70 percent. This would mean going back to the consumption levels of the nineteenth century and is clearly unrealistic. It appears, therefore, that CO_2 levels will continue to rise for at least another hundred years. The CO_2 share of the atmosphere was about 335 ppm (parts per million) in 1980, and will almost certainly reach 360 ppm in 2000. It is likely to keep rising by about 1.2 ppm a year throughout the twenty-first century.

Carbon emissions are but part of the syndrome of our already nearly irreversible pollution problem: CFC emissions are another. Chlorofluorocarbons, man-made substances widely used in refrigerators and air conditioners, eat into the layer of ozone in the upper atmosphere. This layer is much needed, since it forms a vital shield against the sun's ultraviolet (UV) rays.

Most scientists believe that even a modest rise in UV radiation could increase the risk of cataracts and skin cancer in humans, and damage crops and other plants. It may also contribute to changes in the world's climate.

Ever since 1985, when scientists realized that an ozone hole had opened over the South Pole, efforts have been made to reach international agreement to phase out the production of CFCs. The 1990 Montreal CFC convention, which set the year 2000 as the target for a complete ban on production, is widely hailed as a triumph of global cooperation in environmental protection. Yet the problem is not as readily overcome as that: Although after 2000 CFC concentration in the atmosphere may no longer rise, ozone destruction will continue for decades more. And even when production is completely halted, the billions of tons of CFCs that have already been produced will continue to seep into the atmosphere.

CFC-caused ozone depletion is more serious than was originally thought. Measurements since the mid-1980s have indicated a faster and greater ozone loss than scientists had predicted at the time. In March 1993, WMO, the World Meteorological Organization, reported that in the winter of 1992/93 ozone levels over northern regions of Europe and Canada fell by an unexpected 20 percent; a month later *Science* magazine reported that satellite readings indicate an average ozone concentration in the upper atmosphere that is 1.5 percent below computer projections.

Further to atmospheric emissions, toxic wastes pose another man-made pollution problem. An estimated 70,000 chemical compounds are currently discharged into air, soil, and water. Many of them are more toxic than their manufacturers claim: New compounds are created faster than public authorities can test them. In the United States, for example, of the 48,000 chemicals listed by the Environmental Protection Agency (EPA), only 1,000 have been tested for acute effects. The world's oceans are a repository of an officially reported— and almost certainly underestimated—200 million tons of sewage sludge, industrial wastes, and dredged materials annually.

Water is yet another victim of global pollution. Throughout the densely populated regions of the world, clean water is a scarce resource. More than 1.2 billion people lack safe drinking water and 1.4 billion do not have access to proper sanitation. In many areas water is polluted to the point where it cannot regenerate itself. The rate of toxification—due to mining, industrial and human wastes, and the overuse of chemical fertilizers—lengthens the natural cycles of purification with the result that the time it now takes for groundwater to purify by natural means is longer than the average life expectancy of the populations. The imbalance is taking a heavy toll: Dirty water is the world's leading cause of disease and one of the main killers of infants and small children.

Manufacturing industries are a major source of conventional forms of environmental pollution; the armaments industry and power-generating plants create additional forms. There are millions of metric tons of radioactive wastes generated each year by nuclear power plants and nuclear weapons-producing facilities. They include plutonium, a by-product of burning uranium in conventional reactors, the most toxic radioactive substance known. There are also large quantities of irradiated fuel rods, radioactive liquids, and low-level toxic wastes. Most of these dangerous wastes are in short-term storage, and are often leaking. Though such substances will remain toxic for millennia, no country has built facilities for long-term toxic-waste storage; even the best facilities are seldom safe for more than 100 years. At the same time, several countries still pursue plutonium-based energy policies. The policy contemplated by Japan may be the most threatening: It would result in the production of more of this deadly substance than there is currently held in all of the world's nuclear arsenals.

Pollution from toxic wastes affects the entire global biosphere, but local contamination levels vary from the worrisome to the acutely dangerous. The most dangerous region in the world is the former Soviet republics, especially Russia, Belarus, Ukraine, and Kazakhstan. Some of the worst problems are caused by the huge Mayak nuclear weapons complex in the South Urals. Nuclear waste tanks have been known to explode at Kyshtym, while wastes have been routinely dumped into rivers and lakes near Chelyabinsk. The waters of Lake Karachai are reputed to be the most polluted and dangerous on earth.

Another problem area is the Arctic sea region: Nuclear submarines abandoned at Novaya Zemlya are likely to be leaking radioactive materials, and Russia continues to dump low-level nuclear wastes into the sea. It is estimated that there are 6,000 tons of spent nuclear fuel in the former Soviet republics, and tens of thousands of fuel assemblies in Russian nuclear submarines.

The cost of cleanup will be prohibitive not only for Russia, but for all of Eastern Europe and Central Asia. In the United States alone, cleanup at nuclear weapons plants may take thirty years and cost $150 to $250 billion. Elsewhere cleanup appears to be beyond the realm of possibility; the best that may be achieved is to reduce wastes and pollution to "acceptable" levels. Just what is acceptable is highly problematic, however, seeing that some of the wastes kill on contact and others have a known capacity to cause cancer, sterility, immune disease, birth defects, and genetic mutation.

Climate. There are forms of pollution—industrial and urban pollution, rather than nuclear wastes—that have an additional side effect: They change the thermal and chemical equilibrium of the Earth's atmosphere. They thus alter weather patterns. The most important triggers of climate change are the so-called greenhouse gases: carbon dioxide, methane, ozone, chlorofluorocarbons, and oxides of nitrogen. Though the emission rates of various greenhouse gases may now grow slower, they are not likely to diminish. Consequently atmospheric concentrations will increase and a warming trend will raise average annual temperatures.

The climatological record shows a continuing buildup of the greenhouse gases throughout this century, at a rate near 1 percent annually. The record also shows an annual mean rise of global surface air temperatures of about 0.5° C since 1905, with a reversal to lower values in the 1950s, sixties, and early seventies. Although the variability of temperature within given years has been high, in the 1980s there was an overall acceleration of warming. Current global temperatures reach up to the maximum values attained since the last ice age 9,000 years ago.

The overall increase during this century is consistent with predictions from the more conservative computerized climate models. Somewhat more than the observed warming could have resulted from the increase of greenhouse gases in the atmosphere, but the warming that did result could not have had natural sources. Observed variations in the quantity of solar radiation reaching the Earth—the so-called solar constant—could not account for more than about one degree plus or minus in the average values of global temperature. For this reason it is also futile to pin hopes on the solar constant; even if it did decrease somewhat, it is not likely to significantly offset the global warming due to the accumulation of atmospheric greenhouse gases.

In all likelihood, global warming will continue. A 1991 projection by IIASA (the International Institute of Applied Systems Analysis) showed a spread of probable warming between 4.5° C and almost 10° C in the year 2050, and 12° to 15° C by the end of the next century. These projections were preliminary and probably high: They did not include the time lags caused by the thermostatic effect of the deep oceans. It is more reasonable to believe that global averages will increase somewhere between 0.5° and 2.5° C in 2030, and will move up to 3.6° C, and possibly 4.5° C, by 2050. Temperatures will rise more in the north than in the south, and even at conservative estimates are bound to produce significant changes in precipitation.

The long-term effects of climate change on the global ecolgoy, economy, and settlement patterns are still unclear. Efforts by scientists to connect world climate models with local precipitation models are in their infancy: The existing models do not give adequate estimates in regard to amounts of local rainfall and, more important, do not disclose how rainfall is converted into runoff, groundwater, and evaporation. It is nevertheless more than likely that in many parts of the world the warming trend would have negative effects on agriculture. The monsoon may miss the Indian subcontinent and irrigate the deserts of central Asia; tropical Africa may dry out as water falls on the sands of the Sahara. The permafrost of northern Canada and Siberia may melt, but this would expose soils not able to sustain intensive cultivation. A doubling of the greenhouse gases in the atmosphere could raise temperatures in Canada by 4° to 6° C and in the United States by 6° to 8° C. But already a 4.5° C warming would transform the Midwest into a dust bowl and drop the water level in Colorado. While Alaskan fish catches would increase due to warmer currents, California, deprived of the waters of the Colorado, would be unable to irrigate its vineyards and orchards. Lake Michigan would evaporate, and the wetlands of Louisiana would be lost to the sea.

Though many uncertainties persist, we may be assured that the effects of global warming on rainfall and sea level have serious consequences for human settlements and our life-supporting eco- and agro-systems. Views that such effects will be negligible in the long run are naive, politically motivated, or simply irresponsible.

Deforestation. In many parts of the world changes in the climate impair the growth of trees. Ecologists estimate that on the average 3,000 square meters (32,000 square feet) of forest are lost every day, due in part to destructive human behavior. Slash-and-burn cultivators, loggers, cattle ranchers, and settlers seeking fresh land are responsible for the loss of about 10 million hectares of tropical forests per year; another 10 million hectares of forest are degraded by subsistence cultivators, fuelwood gatherers, charcoal makers, and small-scale loggers. As a result, deforestation is becoming worldwide. The planet had an estimated 6.2 billion hectares of forests when serious human interventions began with the Neolithic Revolution; today it has about 4.2 billion.

Climate change, however, remains the major factor in the life of forests. If tropical vegetation zones become more arid, the great rain forests of Central Africa and Brazil will die: In the tropics trees do not tolerate more than small variations in temperature and rainfall. Scientists at the IIASA Biosphere Project found that the critical thresholds of aridity would be reached if atmospheric CO_2 levels actually doubled. In that case the tropical rain forests, even the boreal forests that ring the Northern Hemisphere from Scandinavia to Canada and Northern Siberia, would be affected. With a doubling of atmospheric carbon dioxide, up to 40 percent of the boreal forest belt would be unable to support the current species of trees.

The problem is that, given long (thirty-, fifty-year-plus) tree growth cycles, a rapid warming trend would not allow forests to regenerate by themselves: There would not be enough time for replacement species to immigrate. Even reforestation would be rendered difficult, since the seedlings of the current species would die before reaching maturity, while the seedlings of species more adapted to the coming conditions could not survive in the present climate.

The loss of more than a third of the Earth's tree cover is a major cause of ecological disequilibrium. Trees absorb CO_2, conserve water in the soil and prevent erosion, and shelter

myriad plant, animal, and insect species essential for biological diversity. Tropical forests, which cover only 7 percent of
the land surface, harbor 50 percent or more of the existing species of plants and animals. Clearing them may condemn up to
a million species to extinction within the next ten years alone.

The diminution of the forested areas and the accumulation
of CO_2 in the atmosphere form a self-reinforcing feedback
loop. As trees die, the carbon dioxide contained in them is released into the environment, where it conflates with CO_2 emissions due to various human and technological activities, such
as the burning of wood and other fossil fuels. As much as
25 percent of the current carbon dioxide emissions are likely
to originate in forest dieback: Dead trees release CO_2. Since
living trees absorb it, the accumulation of CO_2 in the biosphere is vastly accelerated by a worldwide loss of forests.

In addition to triggering a CO_2-based vicious cycle, deforestation destroys upland watersheds. In the developing
countries as a whole, around 160 million hectares of upland
watersheds have been seriously degraded over the past three
decades. Watersheds, however, are important elements of
ecological balance: They influence rainfall patterns, regulate
water flow and entire hydrological cycles, and provide habitats
for a great variety of plants and animals.

Food. Land-based agriculture is one of the major achievements of human civilization. Yet it has a history of causing environmental damage. When about 70 percent of a given land
area is intensely cultivated, the productivity of the soil tends to
diminish. To maintain yields per area, modern farmers resort
to increasing inputs of fertilizers, irrigation, and mechanical
energy. When these inputs reach excessive levels, the soils collapse. Scientists at the Institute of Photosynthesis and Soil Pa-
thology of the Russian Academy of Sciences estimate that a
similar process of overexploitation and collapse has recurred
over and over again in history. In classical Mesopotamia, for
example, soil collapse is likely to have occurred within one or
two centuries after cultivation reached the critical level.

The prolonged cultivation of tilled lands has rapid and usually unforeseen effects on soil productivity. About two-thirds of the cultivated land in Siberia is threatened with imminent erosion, and one-third of the land in China. The Indian government has officially recognized that about 30 percent of that country's surface area is "impoverished"—that is, unusable for agriculture, forests, and other humanly beneficial purposes.

For most of this century, great increases in food production have been achieved, first by bringing more land under cultivation and then by using more fertilizers on the cultivated lands. Further increases, however, will encounter serious constraints. Irrigation and cultivation costs militate against bringing significantly more land under cultivation, while falling soil productivity on the existing lands can no longer be compensated for by further increments in the use of chemical fertilizers. This means that the energy won from food cannot keep pace with the food-energy needs of the population. Directly or indirectly, the five and a half billion people who now inhabit the planet consume about 40 percent of the solar energy fixed on land, or 50 percent of the solar radiation fixed in biomass when the harvest of the oceans is included. Within the next thirty-five years the world population is expected to double, but there is no known method by which these percentages could be doubled.

Energy. The coming of the fifth wave has yet another major cause: the deepening commercial energy deficiency. Global stress due to lack of adequate energy should hardly come as a surprise: In the last 200 hundred years, about one-half of the world's total fossil energy reserves—the product of 300 million years of solar radiation—has been used up. In this century alone, the human community used more energy than in all of recorded history. The gross energy consumption curve, though flattening, cannot level off: There are too many young people and development-eager societies to permit efficiency measures to cut back on overall production quotas. But the historical rates of increase are not sustainable, even with the most promising alternative energy technologies.

As we know, the classical fossil fuels are in limited supply. Although uncertainties persist regarding the size of the reserves, it is clear that current rates of use would exhaust them within a few generations. Recoverable crude oil reserves are estimated by OPEC at 1 trillion barrels: At the current ratio of production to reserves it would last about 42 years. The reserves of natural gas are put at 124 trillion cubic meters: At current rates of use this would last about 58 years. Coal would last longer: The more than 1 trillion-million tons of it would be enough for some 238 years, although actual use would cause large-scale water shortages. The problem is more urgent, however, than these figures indicate. The burning of all varieties of fossil fuels pollutes the environment, adding to the already critically high CO_2 levels in the atmosphere. There would have to be a switch to nonfossil energy technologies at the earliest realistic opportunity.

Nonfossil technologies have their own constraints, however. Hydroelectric power is limited to mountainous regions with rapidly flowing rivers. While more efficient water mills could harness the flow of slower and smaller streams, in the global context their yield could not be significant. Solar technologies face the problem of the intermittence and diffusion of their energy source. Powering such urban-industrial complexes as the New York–Washington or the Tokyo–Yokohama area would call for vast fields of solar collectors on the surface of the Earth, or for an entire array of transmitting satellites in geosynchronous orbit.

In its currently employed form, based on nuclear *fission*, atomic energy is not the answer. Projections show that even if only the presently operating coal-fired power stations were to be replaced by fission-based power stations under the assumption of a moderate growth in energy demand, for about thirty-eight years at least one new nuclear reactor of average capacity would have to be pressed into service every 2.4 days. China alone would have to have an estimated 785 nuclear reactors if its population were to live at Western living standards. But the available technologies are hazardous: Reactor safety is a problem even under peaceful conditions. Under conditions of unrest, with potential terrorist acts and war actions, the problems soon assume unacceptable dimensions. Breeder reactors and reprocessing plants, while extending the energy output from fissional materials, add to the risks: The plutonium cycle and the liquid sodium cooling system have major destructive potentials.

Unlike nuclear fission, the technologies of nuclear *fusion* are comparatively safe, producing far less radiation and using ordinary sea water rather than such rare and hazardous substances as uranium and plutonium. The problem that fusion faces is commercial application at a cost-competitive level. "Hot" fusion technologies are not far beyond the break-even point, where the amount of energy won in the process does not exceed the energy that goes into running it; cold fusion, if not simply a hoax, is still a distant prospect.

The constraints that limit nonfossil energy technologies should not lead us to the pessimistic conclusion that safe and sustainable energy sources cannot be developed and tapped in coming years. We need merely to remember that the Sun sends to the Earth some 178,000 terawatts (that is, 178,000 billion kilowatts) of energy per year. Of this staggering amount, only 0.02 percent (about 40 terawatts) is converted by Nature into biomass—the rest heats the oceans, the atmosphere, and the continents, or is reflected back into space. A higher, more efficient use of solar radiation could cover all of humanity's foreseeable energy needs. For example, if only the solar energy falling on the territory of a country the size of Germany would be 10 percent exploited, current world energy consumption would be covered not once, but 80 times over. Of course, the relevant technologies—as already noted—have limitations and constraints. The consensus among energy experts is that about 12 billion kilowatts (that is, 12 terawatts) of nonfossil and also nonnuclear energy could be commercially generated by harnessing nature's solar, wind, wave, tidal, hydro, biomass, and geothermal energies. This is not as much as the current global energy use, which, relying 80 percent on fossil sources, is estimated at 13.5 terawatts. However, advances in energy efficiency could drop the global consumption rate without reducing its benefits. With proper technologies and management, a global supply of 12 terawatts could go as far as 20 or even 24 terawatts would go today.

The uneven distribution of energy consumption will, of course, remain a problem. The industrialized countries now consume more than 7.5 kw of commercial energy per person per year, while in the underdeveloped countries the average per capita consumption does not exceed 1.1 kw. If 12 terawatts (which is 12 billion kw) would be evenly distributed, a world population of 6 billion people would be limited on the average to using 2 kw per person. In the industrialized countries such a drop is most unlikely: Even political will and the finest technologies in the world could not support today's material lifestyles with a consumption of less than about 3 kw per capita. Consequently, if by the end of the century people everywhere are to use safe and sustainable energy sources and live at the material standard of today's "rich," some 18 TW of nonfossil and nonnuclear energies would have to be on hand. As this is hardly feasible, either a persistent reliance on fossil and fission technologies, or a considerable level of unevenness in energy use, is likely to persist into the twenty-first century.

PRINCIPAL CAUSES OF THE FIFTH WAVE

- There are about 100 million acts of sexual intercourse every day, of which about 910,000 result in conception. Consequently, the net daily growth in the world population is more than a quarter of a million human beings;

the annual increment is 97 million. If the population keeps growing at this rate, in the year 2000, 79 percent of the world population will be in the third world, and in the year 2020, 83 percent.

- Population growth in the world is geometrical, progressing as the ratio of 1 to 2, to 4, to 8. . . . But food and other life necessities can increase at the most at an arithmetical ratio, as 1 to 2, to 3, to 4. . . .

- The rich-poor gap continues to widen: currently the richest 20 percent of the world population earns 150 times more than the poorest 20 percent.

- There are more than 100 million Africans with acute food deficiency, 60 million are on the edge of starvation, and nobody knows how many millions die of AIDS. In South Asia 200 million people live permanently in the shadow of famine and disease.

- Since the beginning of this century, an estimated 250 million people have left their native lands, searching for a better life or merely for ways to survive. About 12.5 million roam sub-Saharan Africa alone. During the 1990s at least 15 million illegal immigrants may cross the border from Mexico to the United States, and another 30 million by 2020; a similar stream may develop from North Africa into Europe.

- Of the total flow of investments, in 1990 $163 billion went to the industrialized countries and $30 billion to the developing ones. Three-fourths of this small slice went to ten countries, of which half—Singapore, Hong Kong, Brazil, Mexico, and Argentina—are already industrialized; the forty-two least developed countries received but 0.7 percent of third-world capital investment.

- The world's military establishments employ more than 2 percent of the global work force and cost an estimated $1,000 billion annually. Some 150 states now maintain their own armies.

- A child coming into the world in the United States and living for eighty-two years will consume an estimated 56 million gallons of water, 21,000 tons of gasoline, 100,000 pounds of steel, and the wood of 1,000 trees.

- More than 1.2 billion people lack safe drinking water. And 1.4 billion do not have access to proper sanitation. Dirty water is the world's leading cause of disease and one of the main killers of infants and small children.

- About 7 billion tons of carbon dioxide are pumped into the atmosphere each year, some 45 percent of it by twenty-four industrialized states. If, as agreed, CO_2 emissions were to be stabilized at 1990 levels, industrialized states would have to cut "business as usual" emissions by 44 percent between now and the year 2050. Such reductions would entail nearly unbearable economic costs but would produce only an 11 percent worldwide reduction if countries such as China and India continued to increase their own emissions by the current annual average of 3.7 and 3.9 percent.

- A doubling of CO_2 and other greenhouse gases in the atmosphere would ultimately raise temperatures in Canada by 4° to 6° C, and in the United States by 6° to 8° C. Already a 4.5° C warming would transform the Midwest into a dust bowl and drop the water level in Colorado, depriving California of irrigation water.

- A doubling of atmospheric CO_2 would also lead to the disappearance of the great tropical rain forests, and up to 40 percent of the boreal forest belt that now rings the Northern Hemisphere from Canada to Siberia and Scandinavia. The disappearance of tropical forests, which cover only 7 percent of the land surface but harbor 50 percent or more of the existing species of plants and animals, could condemn up to a million living species to extinction within the next ten years alone.

- Irradiated fuels, radioactive liquids, and low-level toxic wastes are generated each year by nuclear power plants and nuclear weapons–producing facilities; there are 6,000 tons of spent nuclear fuel in the former Soviet republics alone, and tens of thousands of fuel assemblies in Russian nuclear submarines. These substances are mostly in short-term temporary storage, which is often leaking. Though they will remain toxic for millennia, even the United States has not built facilities for toxic waste storage that are safe for more than 100 years.

- The industrialized countries consume more than 7.5 kw of commercial energy per person per year, while the average per capita energy consumption in the underdeveloped countries does not exceed 1.1 kw.

- In the last 200 years about one-half of the world's total fossil energy reserves—the product of 300 million years of solar radiation—has been used up. Alternative energies at the required level are not easy to come by: Given but a moderate growth in world energy demand, if the presently operating coal-fired power stations were to be replaced by fission-based generators, one new nuclear reactor would have to be pressed into service every 2.4 days, for the next thirty-eight years.

THE FIFTH WAVE SYNDROME

Global stress, the fifth shock wave likely to descend on the human community in this century, has multiple causes. This makes it not easy to cope with because we have to attack each of its many causes on its own. But we also have to take cross impacts into account. There are many interactions and hence cross impacts among the stress factors: They tend to form vicious cycles that feed back to, and thus aggravate, one another. Take only the following instances:

- The burning of fossil fuels, deforestation, climate change, energy use, and the impact on agriculture are directly linked. Fossil fuel–based pollution creates acid rain, and acid rain kills trees. As trees die, the carbon stored in them is released into the environment. This adds to the CO_2 content of the atmosphere, reinforcing existing pollution and triggering climate change, which in turn promotes forest dieback and depresses agricultural productivity.

- Urban concentration, industrial complexes, misused or inappropriate technologies, and unsuitable forms of energy create pollution, cause deforestation, trigger climate change, and reduce world agricultural production. Combined with an unrelenting growth in human numbers, they create an unsustainable load on the environment.

- Degraded environments aggravate the condition of the world's poor, and poverty depresses the chances of health and well-being of future generations. Women and children are often the most affected: In many societies when food is scarce, small children and women, including expectant mothers, are the last to be fed. Babies born of undernourished mothers are weaker and less viable than healthy babies. If they continue to be undernourished in the critical first years of life they may suffer physiological effects, including permanent brain damage. Undernourished children born of starving mothers could find themselves handicapped in adolescence and adulthood, especially when confronted with the necessity of coping with the vicissitudes of a poverty-constrained life.

- As economies stagnate while populations grow, it is inevitable that employment opportunities should vanish and cities become overcrowded. People pushed to the edge of subsistence may leave their native land and emigrate. Mexicans are already streaming across U.S. borders, and transborder migration is expected to swell in coming years. Another wave is developing at the southern shores of the Mediterranean as North Africans try their luck in Europe. A third major wave could advance from China into the thinly settled regions of Siberia; others would follow if the greenhouse effect triggers coastal flooding. Massive population movements, involving as many as a billion people, would produce major stresses and a high level of social, economic, and political tension. They would threaten stability and peace both within and among the world's nations.

Unless decisive and timely action is taken, the processes that now stress the globalized society/nature system will intensify and create a shock wave that will foreclose a successful completion of the grand transition. It will thus jeopardize the future of all people and societies. This is not in anybody's interest. Averting the fifth wave—or at least mitigating its effects—is the first vital cause shared by the whole of the human family.

3

A Short Catalogue of Obsolete Beliefs and Misguided Practices

Our difficulty is that we are just emerging from a technological entrancement. During this period the human mind has been placed within the narrowest confines it has experienced since consciousness emerged from its Paleolithic phase.

U.S. CULTURAL HISTORIAN THOMAS BERRY

Overpopulation, poverty, militarization, environmental degradation, climate change, food and energy shortages, and all the other processes that make for global stress are not fated: They are the result of human actions. Therefore, they will *respond* to human actions—provided that the beliefs and values that inspire the relevant actions are rooted in a broader vision. It is not, after all, as if measures to relieve global stress did not exist: They include the destruction of weapons of mass destruction, the elimination of dangerous technologies, the reduction of CO_2 and other greenhouse gas emissions, the reforestation of denuded lands, the prevention of soil erosion, the reduction and cleanup of pollution, the limitation of population growth (especially in the major cities) . . . to mention but the most obvious. The question, however, is whether we will generate the vision to actually *implement* such measures.

Certainly, the patterns of action in today's world are not encouraging. The world community is on the one hand relieved of the specter of superpower confrontation, while on the other it is threatened by ecological collapse. Yet the world's governments spend $1,000 billion a year on arms and the military and only a tiny fraction of this sum on maintaining a livable environment. Even small reductions in military spending could fund major health and literacy programs, create essential infrastructures, and bring marginalized people into the orbit of the modern world economy. But neither "peace dividends" nor other actions to solve global problems have a high priority on the international agenda. It has become commonplace to speak of a lack of political will, or of vested interests preventing real progress beyond the status quo.

What lies at the root of this frustrating state of affairs? An analysis of the dominant (though not always consciously held) values and beliefs of governments, businesses, and entire societies sheds light on this question. We begin with the beliefs modern people typically entertain of their relationship to nature.

The Neolithic Illusion. The values and beliefs shared by most people regarding their relationship to nature go back thousands of years, to the advent of the Neolithic era.

For some 99 percent of the 5 million years since the ancestral line of homo divided from that of tree-living apes, human communities lived in a closed system with the environment. Only the energy of the sun entered this system, and the heat radiated into space left it. Everything else had been cycled and recycled within it. Food and water came from the immediate surroundings, and once they were processed in the bodies of people, they were returned into nature and recycled. Even in death the human body did not leave the ecological system: It entered the soil and contributed to its fertility. Nothing that men and women were, or brought into being, accumulated as "nonbiodegradable" toxins; nothing they did interrupted nature's cycles of generation and regeneration.

The situation changed when groups of early humans

learned to manipulate their natural environment. While tribal groups did not poison nature, the load they placed on it began to increase. The control of fire permitted the stocking of perishable food over longer periods and allowed people to congregate farther from their food supply. The communities grew in number and extended over the continents. They began to transform their immediate surroundings to fit their needs. People were not content to simply gather their food; they learned to hunt, and then to plant seeds and use rivers for irrigation and the removal of wastes. They domesticated dogs, horses, and some species of cattle. These practices enabled them to increase their numbers and extend their dominion. Nourishment began to flow from a purposefully modified environment, while the extra wastes generated by the larger and technologically more sophisticated communities continued to disappear conveniently, with smoke vanishing into thin air and solid waste washing downstream in rivers and dispersing in seas and oceans.

Nature seemed to be effectively open: The environment appeared to be an infinite source of goods and an infinite sink of wastes. Even when a local milieu suffered—from the excessive cutting down of trees and working of soils, for example—there were always virgin lands to conquer and to exploit.

In the Near and Middle East, this "Neolithic illusion"—that nature is an infinite source of resources and an infinite sink of wastes—was reinforced by the emerging religions. This was not unusual: Otherworldly myths and this-worldly realities always interact and influence each other. There were many precedents. For example, the ancient Sumerian myth of the origin of the world told how the world was delivered from the earth goddess after she was raped by the wind god. Modern observers laughed at the image, until a British scientist placed World War II aerial reconnaissance photos of the area on the plotting board and realized that the meanderings of the dried-up beds of the Tigris and the Euphrates outline a woman's body. Considering that the wind blows off the Persian Gulf between the mouths of the two rivers, and that the heavy silt carried by the rivers builds rapidly to create fertile land, the cosmic creation story turned out to be an accurate symbolic representation of the Sumerians' physical environment.

Even more than describing the physical features of the environment, the beliefs of a people reflect the tenor of life within that environment. In ancient Sumer, existence was harsh: Flash floods washed away irrigation channels and dams, and when they dried up they left fields arid. Not surprisingly, in the Sumerian belief system gods created humans because they themselves did not want to toil in the fields. Humans were slaves to the gods. Sumerian statues picture bowed people, with frightened eyes and prayerful hands.

By contrast the Egyptian myths projected a very different rapport between humans and nature: The local environment was much more benign. Most people had an easy life, with the Nile irrigating the land with dependable regularity, bringing in silt and washing away wastes. The great river made for easy travel downstream, while the prevailing winds from the Mediterranean allowed good sailing upstream. The Egyptians hoped to continue their earthly existence in the afterlife and they prepared for it meticulously: They took to the grave all kinds of artifacts and clothes and, if powerful enough, slaves and chariots as well.

Western culture and civilization, however, was shaped more by the Hellenic and the Hebraic than by the Sumerian and the Egyptian belief systems. Greek gods were pagan deities; there were many of them and they personified every human appetite, including sexual drives both normal and aberrant. They had regular concourse (as well as intercourse) with humans, and even among themselves their behavior was licentious. Hera, Zeus's spouse, connived to seduce her husband into plots he would later regret, while Aphrodite, though the wife of Hephaestus, slept with Mars.

The Greek pantheon symbolized history as experienced by the Greeks: The centaurs recalled the nomadic tribes raiding on horseback from the North. These tribes worshiped sky gods, who were mostly male. The earth goddesses, in turn, were carried over from the myths of the Chtonians, who were sedentary farmers. When the sky gods were married with the earth goddesses, their stormy relationships may have reflected marital conditions in many a Hellenic household.

Different from the humanlike gods and goddesses of the Greeks, Yahweh, the god of the Jews, was a jealous and morally exacting god. Unlike the Greek gods, who demanded virtuosity, Yahweh demanded *virtue* of His people: strict adherence to His Covenant, meaning no worship of other gods and idols and strict obedience to a code of behavior with categorical distinctions between right and wrong. This, too, mapped experienced realities: The Jews were originally a group of small and powerless tribes of nomadic shepherds organized into families and clans. When they wandered into the fertile crescent, they were conquered by different armies and eventually taken to Egypt. After several generations they were led by Moses out of captivity and into the promised land. There, a brief period of political independence under King David and his heirs was followed by further suppression by the Romans. In the resulting Diaspora, adherence to the covenanted monotheism of Moses enabled the dispersed and dominated people to keep together and maintain their identity. Their prophets gave assurance that by living a virtuous and obedient life, a Messiah would come to deliver them to freedom in the promised land.

In contrast to the permissive attitude of the Greeks, the discipline imposed by the strict ethics of the Jews fared well. In the form it was later given by Jesus, the proclaimed Messiah to whom many Jews as well as Romans converted, it weathered the rise and fall of the Roman empire.

While the Judeo-Christian belief system created a closer relationship between humans and their one God, it made for more distance between humans and nature. Humankind was held to be the only species created in the image of God, and the only being with an eternal soul worthy of salvation. The original injunction, to be fruitful and dominate nature, lent support to the Neolithic Illusion. It had thus come about that, while in the East Hinduism and the teachings of Lao-tze and the Buddha regarded humans as an integral part of nature, in the Western world people labored earnestly "to multiply and subdue the earth."

Belief in human mastery over nature persisted through millennia. When faith in divine providence was shaken in Europe—in the fourteenth century the plague known as the Black Death decimated the population, and many wars, including the Hundred Years' War between England and France, brought untold suffering—the Church-dominated culture of the medieval world separated into two streams. One remained centered on faith and religion, seeking redemption by intensifying moral discipline and appealing to the divine powers; the other hoped to gain greater control over the physical world to escape suffering and mitigate pain. The latter movement, though at first spiritually imbued, legitimized independent inquiry into the nature of reality. By the sixteenth century it had evolved into modern science. A century later modern science, in turn, found powerful applications by marrying traditional handicrafts and giving birth to technology. These applications were inspired by Francis Bacon's inductive method, designed to enable humans to "wrench nature's secrets from her bosom" for their own benefit. This basic philosophy later gave rise to the conviction that it is the "white man's burden" to clear the wilderness, and his right to colonize the "savages."

But subduing the Earth was always a two-edged sword. It created food and livelihood for an increasing population, but at the same time it denuded forested lands and made for an arid environment visited by floods and other natural disasters. In the course of the centuries the God of Christian monotheism acquired a severe reputation, requiring frequent interventions of mercy by Jesus, Mary, and a growing number of saints.

As European and American societies proved resourceful in using modern technology, their apparent success obscured the fact that nature is a closed system. Through technological manipulation the environment yielded more produce per acre, and made more acres available for produce. The fact that the load people placed on their environment would be transferred to wider regions, degrading ever more of the Earth's soil, air, and water, had by and large escaped attention.

The illusion of an open ecological system was maintained as long as the immediate environment contained unexploited resources and unfilled sinks. But as the human population grew in number and increased its demands, that image was bound to shatter. It is the fate of our generation to live at the time when it is about to do so.

The Neolithic illusion can no longer be maintained because the load created by the billions of humans who now populate the Earth produces highly visible impacts. We now see and feel the first major constraints on natural resources due to the finiteness of the planet. We experience the first manifest signs of a finite planetary sink as well: The wastes we discard into the environment no longer vanish but come back to plague us and our neighbors. The refuse dumped into the sea does not dissipate in an endless expanse of water but returns to poison marine life and infest the coastline. Even the smoke rising from our homesteads and factories fails to rise and dissolve: The carbon dioxide released by it remains in the atmosphere and interferes with the weather.

Of course, unlike in the past, the people of our generation do not just make fires to cook food and heat their dwellings, and do not discard only their household wastes. We now inject thousands of chemical compounds into the environment, dump millions of tons of sludge and solid waste into the oceans, release billions of tons of CO_2 into the air, and raise the level of radioactivity in air, water, and land. We ingest enough synthetic compounds and absorb enough radiation in our lifetime to turn our burial grounds into depositories of hazardous substances.

The Obsolete Beliefs. For most of this century we ignored the ever-mounting evidence that nature is a closed ecological system. Encouraged by the newfound powers of modern technology, and by the economic payoffs of the colonization of the American West, we held on to the belief that our environment is, if not an infinite source of resources and an infinite sink of wastes, at least a very large source and a very large sink. We believed that with better technologies and the conquest of virgin lands, we could ignore its limitations and go on as we have before.

At last, in the final decade of this century, the evidence that we live in a closed system with nature has become so visible that we can no longer ignore it. We now know that pursuing the path traced in recent decades (a path that, as we have seen, stretches all the way back to the Neolithic) could lead to disaster. Yet as we head toward the twenty-first century, the broader vision, so urgently needed in coping with the fifth wave, has difficulty in materializing. Many people hold on to outdated and now increasingly backfiring beliefs. The following is a brief sample of them:

- In this world it is each person for himself, with the strongest and most resourceful earning rightful privileges.

- An "invisible hand" harmonizes individual and social interests, so that when each does well for himself he also benefits his society.

- The best way to help the poor and the destitute is for the rich to get still richer, since wealth will inevitably trickle down to benefit the downtrodden and uplift them to decent status. (As John Kennedy said, "A rising tide lifts all boats.")

- Science can solve all problems and reveal all that can be known about humanity and the world.

- Facts alone are what count; values, preferences, and aspirations are merely subjective and therefore inconsequential.

- The way to uncover facts is to specialize and learn as much about a few things as possible, leaving other specialists to concern themselves with all the rest.

- If something can be designed and produced for a profit, it should also be marketed, for it is bound to make at least some people happier or better off.

- True efficiency is maximum productivity for each machine, each enterprise, and each human being.

- We can know all we need to know about people by computing the costs and benefits of their activities and resources, allowing at the most for a few quirks of personality and ethnic background.

- All people owe primary allegiance to their country, and all countries (except the few remaining colonies) are unconditionally sovereign and independent nation-states.

- The wealth and power of one's own country must be assured no matter what this means for other peoples, for in this world it is not only each person for himself, but each country for itself.

- Wealth and political power decide what is to be; ideas serve mainly to fill books and make one's conversation more impressive.

- Our responsibilities end with assuring our own welfare—which happily assures also that of our country—and we should let the next generation fend for itself, as ours had to do.

- There are almost inexhaustible riches in the Earth if we only dare to use our technologies to extract them and put them on the market.

- The unrestrained free market system of economic and political organization is vastly superior to all the rest, and it ought to be adopted by all people in this world in their own best interest.

- Human happiness consists in having the latest, most powerful, and comfortable products.

- Having many children speaks well of one's virility, and of one's resourcefulness in supporting a large family.

- Nature and the environment can pretty well take care of themselves, despite the shrill cries of alarm from the "greens" and some intellectuals.

- The real signs of progress are bigger cities with taller buildings, more and bigger factories, larger and more mechanized farms, more and bigger highways, and a greater selection of products in larger and more luxurious shopping centers.

Beliefs such as these reflect the Neolithic illusion. They inspire mistaken perceptions and practices. They appear in the sphere of the economy, in regard to the ecology, as well as in the way institutions frame and handle economic, ecologic, and political issues.

Economic Blind Spots. The rationality of the world economic system has a blind spot that affects all concerns beyond the near term. The rationality employed by business people and decision-makers in the area of the economy legitimizes short-term actions oriented toward maximizing competitiveness and profit, regardless of the medium- and long-term consequences.

The economic policies of most governments remain seriously flawed. As a rule, politicians are reluctant to pursue policies that reduce the ability of national industries to compete and to produce, no matter what the price. They tolerate high levels of environmental degradation through chemical fertilizers, toxic waste dumping, and CFC emission, rather than putting a brake on economic wealth creation by ecologic sanctions and regulations.

A range of flawed policies colors the behavior of governments both in the industrialized and the developing world.

- Advanced industrialized countries, including the United States, often perceive a need to bolster the international competitiveness of their economies by a dominant military presence. They believe that their search for economic security in a highly competitive world requires and therefore legitimizes the maintenance of vast armies and large stockpiles of high-tech weaponry.

- Countries with unused industrial capacity and significant foreign debt, such as Brazil, look to weapons production as a way to cope with trade deficits and increase hard-currency exports.

- Resource-rich developing countries in Latin America, West Africa, and Southeast Asia respond to mounting pressures to obtain foreign currency by shifting economic priorities to targets such as planting cash crops and exporting metals, minerals, timber, and other natural resources, even if this irreversibly depletes their national patrimony.

Individual politicians are not always to blame: Many governments are constitutionally prevented from taking the longer view. In democratic political systems parliamentary cycles are four or five years, and during this time the incumbents must produce results of tangible benefit or risk being booted out of office in the next election. National projects that take a decade or more to pay off are given low priority, if any attention at all. In consequence every electoral cycle begins with a tangle of unsolved problems whose combined impact becomes ever less amenable to quick fixes and ever more difficult to paper over. In a growing number of areas—monetary, economic, ecologic, and social—public statesmanship is turning into crisis management.

The economic blind spot affects the private sector as well: It is especially evident in the operation of financial markets. The "Wall Street syndrome" of investing for assured short-term profit effectively prevents the espousal of wider perspectives. Pressures for short-term payoffs have been increasing in the last few years with the emergence of the institutional investor as a major financial actor. Whereas the private investor often looked at the long-term growth potential of stocks and was influenced by the "green" posture of given firms, the institutional investor has no personal credo other than to provide the rapid and assured payoffs his clients require. In consequence managers of highly endowed mutual and pension funds move around large amounts of money in search of quick returns. This deflects capital from lower-yield projects, even if they would serve sound long-term objectives.

The rationality that still imbues economic policy—the rationality of neoclassical economics—assumes a world of certainty, technological optimism, and a high degree of substitutability for exhaustible resources. Often GNP and other standard economic indicators mask long-term costs and reinforce the illusion of an infinite natural resource base.

Sometimes economic theory suggests that wealth is actually increasing, even as natural resources are diminishing. For example:

- If a country allowed criminality to rise and tried to combat it by setting up a large police force with scores of prisons, it would experience a rise in its GNP. The same would occur if it permitted diseases to spread and invested in doctors and hospitals to fight the outbreaks.

- If a government decided to cut down all its forests and sell them as timber, its accounting books would report that its national wealth had increased.

- This would also occur if a state permitted pollution to become rampant and then fought it by creating incentives for antipollution industries: Economic rationality would hold that it became richer in the process.

According to mainstream economics, the long-term costs of all such activities remain outside the accounting system as "externalities." As a result, factories can pollute rivers as if the waters that flowed past them entailed no costs; power stations can burn coal without calculating the cost of pumping carbon dioxide into the atmosphere; loggers can destroy wildlife and disrupt ecological cycles without factoring the costs into their balance sheets; and farmers can use chemical fertilizers, pesticides, and fuel oil as if the self-regenerating capacity of the soil and the supply of fossil fuels were unlimited.

Standard economic indicators give a false picture of the health of entire economies. For example, the indicator known as the "country risk index" (developed to measure hard currency availability in a country) is used by banks and institutional investors to decide how much money to channel into an economy. In practice this index, prepared annually in New York, is inflated into an arbiter of well-being the world over— with highly questionable consequences. Investors guided by the risk index are encouraged to move into opportunistic countries that earn foreign currency even at the cost of depleting their natural-resource base. They are discouraged from dealing with countries that have modest foreign-currency earnings even if they pursue such forward-looking objectives as upgrading their infrastructure and providing education for their people.

The economic blind spot that channels funds to entire economies in view of quick returns is strongly dysfunctional: Development cannot take off without some form of investment in the future. There must be investment in people: spreading literacy, disseminating relevant and useful knowledge, furthering creativity, and fostering the ability to cope with technology. There also must be investment in infrastructure: creating more adequate habitations and manufacturing plants, better information and communication facilities, and improved roads and port facilities. And there must be investment in environmental sustainability as well: protecting topsoils, reforesting cleared and eroding lands, and developing or importing safe and resource-efficient technologies.

Evidently, all this costs money. Because policies are keyed to the short term, projects dealing with the development of human resources and basic infrastructures and the protection of the environment are underfunded everywhere in the world. In the least developed countries, they are not funded at all.

Ecological Shortsightedness. The problems of flawed economic rationality are aggravated by the retreating yet persistent myopia that still confronts basic ecologic issues. Although the public is fascinated by stories of major ecodisasters, such as the periodically recurring oil spills, attention focuses on the handful of birds and seals that well-meaning people rescue from the oil slick, while the systematic degeneration of the environment through ongoing exploitation, pollution, and misguided technological practices is mostly overlooked. Yet these are the processes that constitute the long-term danger to life and well-being on this planet.

For instance, major infrastructure projects in developing countries often turn out to produce vexing ecological side effects. The most widely publicized among them are those due to the construction of big dams, with enormous investment of money, capital, manpower, and natural resources. The Aswan Dam in Egypt is the most dramatic example. Large populations have been infected by water-borne viruses, hundreds of thousands of people have been displaced, major archaeological treasures have been endangered, and the productivity of vast areas of land has been impaired.

Less widely known ecological "surprises" have occurred on almost all continents:

- States in the Sahel region of Africa have used some of their international development funds to contract with foreign companies to drill wells and to tap underground water in the desert. The aim was to assure dependable supplies of fresh water, but the side effect was the arrival of nomadic tribes with large families and livestock. The nomads settled nearby, and under the pressure of grazing and firewood gathering, the fragile ecosystems of the oases soon collapsed.

- In Indonesia, Green Revolution rice varieties and intensive cultivation lifted domestic rice production to the level of self-sufficiency. But the expanding rice-growing areas push subsistence farmers into the hills, where cultivation produces poor yields and further erodes the already marginal soils.

- In the fertile Cañeta Valley of Peru, the government prompted the introduction of organic insecticides to combat major insect outbreaks. Contractors removed trees to allow the aerial spraying of the fields, and when they completed the treatment it turned out that beneficial insects and birds were removed together with the harmful varieties. Dosages had to be continuously increased over the years, eroding the lands and reducing ecological diversity. In the end, certain species that had not been harmful until then were released from control and became pests, while some of the harmful insects developed resistance to the chemicals. Ten years later, the region was an ecologic as well as an economic disaster.

- Even in highly disciplined China, the policies of the government lead toward the pollution of the atmosphere and the collapse of vast agricultural lands. Overall pollution levels are increasing at the rate of 30 to 40 percent every seven or eight years. While this figure is modest when compared to the growth rate of China's industrialization (the GNP doubles during the same period), it is likely to be unsustainable beyond the present decade and catastrophic in the long term. Yet atmospheric pollution will be increasing as the consumption of coal is going up. Coal consumption is considerable already: Since 1990 China has been burning a full ton of coal a year for every man, woman, and child in the country.

- China's environmental problems are aggravated by the government's insistence on inculcating the virtues of "modernism" in the populace. This encourages such em-

ulative consumer values as the ownership of private cars.
Men and women in Chinese cities dream of having their
own automobiles, and the central government goes along.
It has signed a joint venture agreement with Volkswagen
for an initial manufacturing capacity of 150,000 cars by
1996, which though small by Western standards is more
than five times the number currently produced in China.
And an agreement with Citroën, subsidized by France,
foresees the production of the same number of cars by
the year 2000. Such policies disregard the larger picture.
If every Chinese had but a motor scooter, world oil consumption would go up by 2 billion barrels a day.

- The continuation of current policies threatens a related
  set of problems in China's countryside. Despite the one-
  family/one-child rule, farmers are having a second and
  frequently also a third child, prompted by family tradition and the need for extra hands around the farm.

  The country's population now exceeds 1.15 billion
  and is expected to grow to 1.5 billion before it will stabilize. This is higher by some 300 million (0.3 billion) than
  the maximum population size projected until recently.
  Three hundred million, however, almost equals the entire population of the European Community. While a
  typical Chinese lives more modestly than a typical European, he and she must eat: China's limited lands must
  feed the Europe-sized increment as well. As it is, those
  lands now feed 22 percent of the world's population, although they comprise only 7 percent of the world's cultivated areas.

Permissive population policies are the prerogative of national governments, but obsolete agricultural policies are practiced by agribusinesses as well as governments, and not only in
the developing South. The overuse of lands through the massive use of chemical fertilizers and pesticides is producing soil
erosion in Europe and in Japan, as well as in North America.

One-third of the cropland in the United States is beginning to show a marked decline in productivity.

Progress toward ecologically foresighted policies is hampered by the still rudimentary knowledge of the dynamics that underlie ecologic processes. Whatever understanding is emerging tends to remain the privileged domain of small groups of specialists—ecophilosophers, deep ecologists, social ecologists, ecofeminists, ecotheologians, and others. The advice offered by theoretically inclined experts tends to emphasize their particular viewpoint in the welter of competing views and theories, while the vision of green politicians and lobbies is often too narrow and short term to produce workable solutions. As a result, even though governments are flooded by advice as to how to handle environmental problems, they are confused by conflicts between competing schools of experts and rival political factions. In the end they choose policies that reflect short-term political constraints rather than sound ecologic understanding. What is expedient wins out over what is really needed.

Policy Specialization and Fragmentation. The world's governments manifest yet another syndrome of obsolescence due to the overspecialization and fragmentation of the policy planning and implementation process. Some governments act as if finance can be separated from trade, defense from development, and social justice from the degradation of the environment: They have departments or ministries attempting to cope with each domain separately, often in direct competition with one another. Although much progress has been made in recent years, environmental issues to this day are handled as if they were another policy specialty. Public officials assign deforestation problems to forestry experts, soil erosion issues to soil pathologists, atmospheric pollution problems to chemists, instead of creating integrated task forces in which ecologic issues are treated as organic elements of the principal policy concerns.

Similar specialization reduces the effectiveness of international institutions as well. Financial flows are handled by the World Bank Group, the coordination apparatus established after World War II at Bretton Woods; security issues are assigned to the UN Security Council, and action in regard to the environment is entrusted to UNEP, the UN's environment program and the Rio follow-up bodies. Health issues have their own World Health Organization and children their UNICEF, just as weather has its World Meteorological Organization and the international mail system the International Postal Union.

Even when an issue cuts across the field of competence of several agencies—such as education, which, in addition to UNESCO, is of concern to UNICEF, UNDP, UNFPA, and half a dozen other UN bodies—the separation of mandates encourages bureaucratic narrow-mindedness and infighting. The result is that, instead of joining forces, territories are insistently claimed and jealously guarded, and the available funds are intensely fought for. Within the UN system, the number-one problem remains coordination—not just the ex post facto coordination of policies created in separate divisions and agencies, but the coordination and integration of the entire planning and implementation process so that policies and actions would be mutually reinforcing instead of mutually debilitating.

The long and complex preparations for UNCED, the 1992 "Earth Summit," showed just how fragmented the international community still is. In PrepCom sessions the delegates of the developing countries were drumming the poverty problem and its causes, blaming the global system of exploitation, while the representatives of the industrialized countries tried to hammer out agreements on specialized legal and institutional matters. They treated issues such as toxic waste pollution in soil and fresh water, sewerage and ocean pollution, deforestation, and biotechnology as if they were separate from one another. In regard to the problem of deforestation, the industrialized countries insisted on a convention that would stop or limit the destruction of tropical rain forests by the developing countries, while the developing countries were intent on obtaining free biotechnologies in exchange for any possible concession on forestry limitations. The many nongovernmental organizations preparing for the Rio event had axes of their own to grind, including the status of women and of indigenous peoples, and special problems faced by developing countries in Asia, Africa, and Latin America.

Segmented approaches such as these have become woefully inadequate. Bernard Shaw's witticism about youth being far too precious to be entrusted to young people applies not only to politics, which is too precious to be entrusted to politicans, but also to the economy, to the ecology, and to all spheres of concern in today's interdependent world, all of which are too precious to be left to the care of specialized—and overspecialized—experts and bureaucrats.

Despite the growing popularity of labels and mottos such as "One world or none," "Spaceship Earth," and "Save the Earth," a truly integrated and effective approach to the problems of humanity and the planet still awaits realization. It is high time to divest the governments and peoples of this world of the fallacies of believing in the rationality of short-term economic goals, in infinitely sustaining environments, and in the effectiveness of specialized approaches to complex interdependent problems.

II

THE IMPERATIVES
OF PERCEPTION

4

Acquiring
Evolutionary
Literacy

*Nobody, after all, can know where he is going if he does
not know where he comes from.*
   FRENCH ANTHROPOLOGIST CLAUDE LÉVI-STRAUSS

Given its dangers and its opportunities, life in a grand transition entails responsibility. If we maintain obsolete values and beliefs, we also maintain outdated behaviors. If such failed behaviors are widespread, they can block the entire transition toward a global information age. Our own persistence in outdated modes of thinking and acting contributes to such an unfortunate outcome.

There is, then, both a moral and a practical obligation for each of us to look beyond the surface of events, beyond the plots and polemics of practical policies, the sensationalistic headlines of the mass media, and the fads and fashions of changing lifestyles and styles of work. The call is to feel the ground swell underneath the events and perceive the direction they are taking: to perceive the evolutionary trend as it drives social change in our world. The call is for a new and urgently needed form of literacy—evolutionary literacy.

PERCEIVING THE EVOLUTIONARY TREND

"Pragmatic" people say that all knowledge of trends is spec-
ulative and superfluous; all one needs is the common sense to
cross bridges as one comes to them. This kind of pragmatism
stems from stable times, when almost any strategy had a knack
of succeeding. The attitude that opportunism pays became in-
grained in the postwar period when national and international
markets were expanding, resources were plentiful, and military R&D spilled over and triggered innovation in civilian
manufacturing and communication. Planning and foresight,
which had been needed during the war years, were gladly sur-
rendered.

After all, if things get better and better on their own, there
is no need to look further ahead than one's nose. In the fifties
and sixties leaders in government and business did not worry
whether or not there would be progress; they only tried to
guess what shape it would take. Breakthroughs and innovations would improve the conditions of life year after year, and
with the improvement of the quality of life would come an improvement in the quality of those living.

Throughout the postwar period development was rapid
and seemed assured. A growing economy welcomed entrepre-
neurs, permitting them to grow as the system grew. Then, in
the 1970s and eighties, the economic growth curve flattened
out and opportunity costs increased. Optimistic extrapolations
failed to come true; "limits to growth" appeared on the horizon. Social alienation and anomie rose. Technology produced
unexpected side effects: scares and catastrophes at Three Mile
Island, Bhopal, and Chernobyl; the ozone hole over the Antarctic; recurrent instances of acid rain and oil spills; and wors-
ening environmental pollution in cities and on land. Youth
groups and environmentalists found it necessary, and some
segments of society fashionable, to espouse the pessimistic
view that technological progress is dangerous and should be
halted. Then, in the wake of the surprising transformation of

Eastern Europe and dissolution of the Soviet Union, some people saw fresh meaning in the old adage that history is "just one darn thing after another," while others speculated that it had come to an end altogether.

The debate between the apostles of technologically impelled progress and the Cassandras of technologically triggered doomsday is still in progress. Going beyond its sterile polemics calls for reliable knowledge as to where we are and how we got here. This means learning to see the basic trend that carries us into the future.

Seeing the basic trend means seeing the pattern that underlies manifest events and happenings. It means perceiving the forest through the trees. Well-developed individuals have a penchant for seeing connections between things, for relating things and events one to another. Humanistic psychologist Abraham Maslow said that the healthy mind sees things whole; overspecialization and fragmentation are signs of psychic malfunction. The ability to see unifying patterns is the sign of a healthy, well-developed personality.

There are developments in the natural sciences that can help us see things whole. The new systems sciences, together with evolutionary cosmology and biology, show that the complexity that meets our eye is not the complexity of a mosaic of independent pieces, but the complexity of a symphony or an organism in which every part is intrinsically related to every other; one in which the parts make an irreducible whole. This whole evolves coherently, from the Big Bang 15 billion years ago to the complex yet harmonious order of nature discovered in contemporary science.

Life, too, evolves on this planet. In its more than 4-billion-year time span it evolved from the protocell and cohered into the complex self-regulating system of Gaia, the embracing bio-socio-sphere. Even the social and ecologic systems formed by humans and other organisms evolve; they, too, follow nature's developmental rhythm. History itself is not the record of the arbitrary doings of kings, and of battles won or lost, but of the evolutionary trend exhibited by complex social systems as they grow and interact. This is the trend that brought humanity from the stone age to the industrial age; the trend that is now taking it toward a global information age.

When we understand the evolutionary trend, we discover the logic behind the grand transition, with its informatization and globalization of the world. A closer look at the principal elements of this trend is well worth our while.

THE CHARACTERISTICS OF THE TREND

To grasp the main features of the evolutionary trend we will make use of current scientific concepts such as *bifurcation, chaos, irreversibility,* and *intersystem convergence.* The meaning of these concepts, and their relevance to the grand transition in which we live, will now be briefly outlined.

Bifurcation and Chaos. Bifurcation, and the condition of chaos that it frequently entails, have specific meaning in the sciences. The dictionary meaning of bifurcation is forking off (from the latin *bi,* meaning two, and *furca,* fork), while in the new sciences it describes the uneven, nonlinear nature of evolution in complex systems. Chaos, in turn, signifies disorder in everyday language, while in the sciences it now means a specific variety of order: subtle, complex, and ultrasensitive.

Bifurcations occur when systems are destabilized in their milieu; they then shift from one set of "attractors" to others. (Attractors define the specific pattern traced by the states of a system as it pursues a path along its evolutionary trajectory.) The processes involve the temporary replacement of stable "periodic" or "point" attractors with unstable "strange" or "chaotic" attractors.

The new discipline of nonequilibrium thermodynamics applies the mathematical simulations of chaos theorists to energy-processing systems in the real world. Real-world systems exist, like vortices in a stream of water, in a state of nonequilibrium within an enduring energy flow. The condition of nonequilibrium signifies the presence of energy concentrations and chemical gradients: It means that the systems are permanently "wound up," having free energy at their disposal. This condition physicists denote with the term "negative entropy."

If fluctuations within or outside a negentropic system upset its delicate energy balance, the system becomes chaotic:

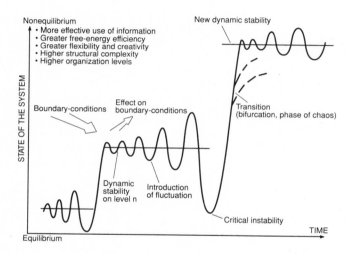

When growing fluctuations upset the dynamic stability of a system, its stable point of periodic attractors can no longer maintain it in its established state; chaotic attractors appear and with them an interval of transition hallmarked by transitory chaos. When the system achieves a new state of dynamic stability, the chaotic attractors of the bifurcation epoch give way to a new set of point or periodic attractors. These attractors maintain the system in a condition far from thermodynamic equilibrium, with more effective use of information, greater efficiency in the use of free energies, greater flexibility (and, in human systems, creativity), as well as greater structural complexity on a higher lever of organization.

Its periodic and point attractors give way to chaotic attractors. If and when the system regains dynamical balance, its unstable chaotic attractors yield to a new set of stable periodic and point attractors.

With concepts such as bifurcation and chaos, leading-edge science helps us deepen our understanding of the current transition from national industrial societies to a globally interconnected information-based socioeconomic system. We realize that this is an evolutionary process that is interspersed with what we have called shock waves. Scientists would call them "cascades of bifurcations." Each cascade—or shock wave—begins with the destabilization of the existing system and the emergence of some form of chaos. Chaos, in turn, gives birth to radically new possibilities: to bifurcations in the evolutionary trajectory of chaos-bound societies. This is what happened in czarist Russia, in the Weimar Republic, worldwide at the end of World War II, and in Gorbachev's Soviet Union.

The first major shock wave of this century was the October Revolution that brought Lenin and the Bolsheviks to power. This was the twentieth century's first "cascade of bifurcations." The second cascade began with the rise of Hitler's war and propaganda machine. The third cascade was launched at the end of World War II, as the freshly liberated colonies became the formally sovereign but in fact dependent states of the third world. The fourth cascade unfolded then as the policy of glasnost led to the collapse of the Soviet world empire.

Today, a new cascade of bifurcations—the fifth wave—is about to reach us. Its causes are overpopulation, poverty, waste and pollution, militarization, and the rest of the factors we have described in Chapter Two. It will spell a new bifurcation in the evolution of human societies, but what shape this transformation will take is not predetermined. It is up to us.

Irreversibility. Change in the way people work with one another and relate to their environment—that is, "technological change" in the current, broad interpretation of technology—

has been the principal engine of development in the span of recorded history. It is still that today, indeed more than ever. Technological change is a characteristic feature of the evolutionary trend. We should review its main features as they pertain to our crucial times.

The first thing to note about technological change is that it is generally irreversible. Whatever its nature, the direction of such change is always from the hoe to the plow, and not the other way around. Even if many procedures are invented, only those that represent an improvement in the effectiveness or efficiency of some procedure are actually adopted and handed down. The irreversibility of technological change has held true throughout history, from the fire and the wheel to the steam engine and the jet airplane. It continues to hold for the solar cell, the integrated circuit, and the laser.

The technologies of the stone age were limited to kindling and to some extent controlling fire, and to making and using tools such as the ax, the dagger, and various implements for cutting and scraping. When during the upper Paleolithic *Homo erectus* evolved into *sapiens,* new technologies were developed, making more effective use of the human hand and its counterposed thumb. Basic raw materials came to include bone, ivory, and antler, and to a lesser extent shells and clay, in addition to stone, wood, and skin. Tool use expanded from drilling, scraping, threading, and cutting to include twisting, grinding, and pressure flaking.

Some 8,000 to 10,000 years ago, during the Neolithic, new technologies were invented, such as hammers with a hole for handles, and saws, daggers, knives, and sickles. They were improved by gouging, carving, polishing, and grinding. When agriculture became the principal mode of food production, harder, stronger, and more durable tools were needed, and in time improved implements appeared. They were tools made of metal—first copper, then bronze, and later iron.

Except for reliance on steel rather than iron, the 8,000 years that separated the Neolithic Revolution from the Industrial

Revolution witnessed relatively few changes in basic agricultural tools: the sickle, the hoe, the chisel, the saw, the hammer, and the knife continued in use. Real changes occurred mainly in regard to new techniques of irrigation and the introduction of new plant varieties. Then, in the nineteenth century, the Industrial Revolution brought a battery of new technologies on the scene, led by the newly discovered power of steam. It soon shifted the focus of development from agriculture to industry.

The first industrial breakthroughs occurred in Great Britain in textiles. Innovations in spinning cotton stimulated a chain of related inventions that led to the emergence of machines capable of factory-based mass production. Industrial development spread from textiles to iron, as cheaper cast iron replaced more expensive wrought iron. Closely on the heel of innovations in the machine-tool industry were developments in the chemical industry. By the middle of the nineteenth century Britain was a major manufacturing power, followed closely by Germany, France, and the United States. The structures of Western societies transformed from the agricultural to the industrial mold.

In the course of the twentieth century a new type of technological change has been replacing reliance on massive energy and raw-material inputs with the more intangible factor known as information. A growing quantity of information has come to be stored on optical discs, communicated by fiber optics, and processed by computers governed by sophisticated programs with millions of operations per second. In consequence the contemporary world has become rapidly informated.

Even if a given technological change has been motivated by considerations such as efficiency, power, and profit, its unwitting effect is—and always has been—the evolution of the structures of society. Every technological change triggers changes in the social structure in which it occurs. The new technologies are no exception: The large and dense flows of information and the proliferating channels of communication make for mutual adjustment and accommodation among contemporary societies. This process unfolds before our very eyes: The contemporary world, as we have seen, is in the midst of a vast transition keynoted by accelerating informatization and globalization.

Intersystem Convergence. Convergence among tribes, communities, and societies has been an enduring feature of the social evolution of humanity. This process sets forth in history a similar process occurring in nature. There, organic species and populations converge within embracing ecologies, and the ecologies themselves converge within the self-regulating systems and cycles of the biosphere. In history, convergence brings together tribes, clans, villages, and provinces in progressively more complex and diversified social, economic, and political systems. The archaic empires of China and India, for example, incorporated villages and regional communities in subcontinental administrative structures; the classical Roman Empire was built of numerous city-states, regions and provinces under the aegis of Pax Romana; and the European empires of the modern age consisted not only of villages, towns, and provinces in the home countries but also of strings of overseas colonies.

Today, the hierarchical structures created by convergence through political power is replaced by more democratic structures produced through participation and information-sharing. Every contemporary state consists of metropolitan centers and rural areas with surrounding villages and towns. Federated states consist of politically and socioeconomically integrated states, republics, or provinces administered by regional governments that in turn are overseen and coordinated by the national capital.

Convergence among societies can temporarily reverse. Such a reversal occurred in the middle of this century, when the hierarchical empires of European nation-states disintegrated and gave rise to strings of newly independent nations. But convergence soon moves forward again. It did so as of the 1960s, as many of the newly created nation-states began to enter into regional groupings and alliances with one another. In the eighties participatory convergence moved into high gear with the creation of subregional and regional free trade zones, economic communities, mutual security blocs, and other forms of economic and political association.

Currently the slow but inexorable creation of a federated structure in the "new Europe" expresses intersystem convergence, much like the ongoing and equally difficult integration

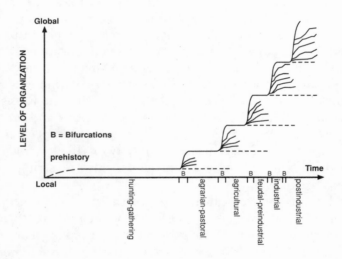

Throughout the span of recorded history, human societies have converged to progressively higher organizational levels. The process began with the hunting-gathering tribes of the Stone Age and currently culminates in the coming of societies globally integrated in the emerging information age. Each bifurcation, driven mainly by the widespread adoption of basic technological innovations, has impelled societies toward more complex, more embracing levels of organization. Today, the widespread adoption of the new information and communication technologies drives the process to the global level.

of North American economies through NAFTA, and of other national states and regional economies in the Asia-Pacific area. A strongly interacting information-based socioeconomic system is taking shape before our eyes.

Bifurcation and chaos, irreversible change, intersystem convergence, and the resulting nonlinear drive toward structure and complexity hallmarked the development of human societies throughout the span of recorded history. In modern times the process accelerated, and in postwar years it became vertiginous. Societal complexity mushroomed; technologies became vastly effective and efficient in exploiting the planet's free-energy sources; and national states, while racked by tensions, were brought together within a variety of economic, social, and military alliances. The convergence of today's nations and economies will culminate in coming years with the integration of nationally based industrial societies within a global-level information-based socioeconomic system— provided that it is not blocked by the intensification of global stress—the fifth shock wave of this century.

The grand transition is not an accident. It is part of the evolutionary dynamic in nature, and notwithstanding its shocks and surprises, it drives toward completion. Only the cascade of bifurcations of the fifth wave can reverse it. But if that wave runs out of control, more would cease than the transition: The entire adventure of life and civilization on this planet would reach an untimely end.

Understanding the main features of the evolutionary trend is the basis for understanding the shocks and surprises that beset our epoch of transition. This understanding, in turn, is the sine qua non for coping with the shocks that are yet in store for us.

Evolutionary knowledge is essential for the responsible governance of modern societies, the management of globe-girdling corporations, and the choices of personal lifestyles. Familiarity with the dynamics of evolution has become part of the literacy of the age.

5

Thriving With Cultural Diversity

Diversity is basic to all things in nature and the human world. A symphony cannot be made of one tone or even played by one instrument; a painting must have many shapes and perhaps many colors; a garden is more beautiful if it contains flowers and plants of many different kinds. A multicellular organism cannot survive if it is reduced to one kind of cell; even sponges evolve cells with specialized functions. And more complex living things have cells of a great variety, with a great variety of functions.

A human community, too, must have members that are different from one another in personality, age, and sex; even in color and creed. Only then can its members perform the tasks that each do best, and complement each other so that the whole formed by them can grow and develop.

The world community as well, has diversity but this diversity is in danger of being flattened. Just as the diversity of nature is threatened by cultivating only one or a few varieties of crops and husbanding only a handful of species of animals, so the diversity of today's world is endangered by the domination of one, or at the most a few, cultures. Cultural diversity in the world is just as essential as diversity in nature and in art. The globalized and informated world that is our evolutionary destiny cannot be viable unless it maintains essential elements of the diversity that has hallmarked human communities since homo first emerged from the trees.

A MULTICULTURAL PLANET

The integrity of the world's cultures is the key to diversity in the world community. Culture is a fundamental element of human life and social existence. The way people lived always has been shaped by what they believed, and what they believed always has depended on how they looked at the world—that is, on their culture. The world is never seen "as it is," in its pristine purity. We see it only through our conceptions and preconceptions, and these are culturally determined. The perceived world, anthropologists and psychologists tell us, is a product of culture: It is "culturally constructed." The danger is that it will soon be uniformly constructed. This would wipe out the rich legacy of the world's great cultural traditions.

The cultures of humanity have evolved over millennia. At the dawn of history, the early cultures saw the world in an atavistic fashion: Not only people, but also animals and plants were believed to have souls; all of nature was alive. A watering hole in the savannah inspired awe for the spirits and forces of nature and for the souls of the dead; a deer appearing in the midst of human settlements was the spirit of an ancestor drawn back to his kinfolk; thunder was a sign from a primordial Mother or an omnipotent Father.

In the course of time human communities evolved and refined their culture-based perceptions. The classical cultures of Greece replaced myth with reasoning: Their world was seen through the prism of natural philosophy, exhibiting a rational pattern of growth from disorder to order; from chaos to cosmos. Later, in the sixteenth and seventeenth centuries, modern science arose in Europe and laid the foundations for a different world-construction. Seen through the prism of early modern science, the world was a giant machine that, once set into motion, performed to the end of time, guided by Newton's precise laws of motion.

Modern science has undergone further "revolutions" in this century, beginning with the one launched by Einstein. But in the meanwhile it has given birth to modern technology. By now this technology-imbued scientific—or pseudoscientific—culture has spread to all corners of the world. All other cultures face the decision whether to open up to the technological culture of the West or close themselves off and value their native ways of living, acting, and worshiping.

In many parts of the world, resistance to Western cultural domination is growing. In the southern half of the Americas, for example, a new brand of cultural nationalism has been emerging. Latin Americans resent their dependence on North America, and also resent being receivers rather than producers of the cultural currents that shape the contemporary world. Foreign cultural domination is an agonizing issue for educated Arabs as well, who perceive it as an element of Western hegemony vis-à-vis their own countries. They, too, find themselves at the passive end of an intercultural dialogue that links them almost exclusively with Western Europe and North America.

India and the countries of South Asia have had prolonged contact with British culture and, though they admire and assimilate many of its traits, have become keen on protecting their own cultural heritage. Russia's historical background has made for profound ambivalence regarding Western culture, and this attitude persists to this day. Its main elements are admiration for the achievements of the West, in technology as well as in high culture, and fear that these achievements will overwhelm the Russian cultural heritage and the identity it bestows on people. Admiration mixed with fear exists also in the young nations of sub-Saharan Africa. African leaders, though often avid consumers of industrial culture, are increasingly intent on fortifying the African cultural heritage in order to confirm their national and racial identity.

The spread of Western technological culture has threatened cultural diversity in the world, but it has not wiped it out. The great cultural traditions still provide people with different ways of seeing, valuing, and acting. This fact is seldom appreciated: Most people in industrialized societies believe that everybody sees the world more or less the way they do. Yet cultural diversity penetrates deeply into people's thinking and acting, shaping worldviews, values, and patterns of behavior. It deserves to be better recognized and valued.

Let us take Latin Americans, for example. The people of that continent are diverse among themselves, but they all have a highly developed sense of spirituality. This has historical roots: The transcendentalist elements of Latin culture date back to the fifteenth century. Throughout the South American continent the Catholic scholasticism of the European middle ages was more than a monastic philosophy: It was a way of perceiving the world that governed every aspect of public and private life.

In both theological doctrine and everyday practice, the people of Latin America were taught that happiness is tied to the sacred vehicle of grace, which in turn is the exclusive prerogative of the Catholic Church. Subservience to ecclesiastical authority, like subservience to God and King, became axiomatic in people's thinking and morality. Even when the colonial epoch drew to a close, no accommodation took place between the scholastic legacy and modern scientific thought. In consequence the southern half of the Americas never evolved the this-worldly orientation that is typical of its northern half. Anglo-Saxon pragmatism, rooted in the application of the concepts and methods of the natural sciences to the material spheres of life, has never taken hold in Latin America.

Though in a different form, transcendentalism is also a feature of the Hindu and Buddhist cultures of the Indian subcontinent, while in the Muslim culture it combines with monotheism and mysticism. The indigenous cultures of Black Africa always have been spiritualist and animistic, and these elements have not been vanquished either by the zeal of Christian missionaries or by the spread of consumerism.

The oriental mind preserves its own particular logic. The great cultural circle that radiated from China during the last millennium was shaped by the naturalism of Lao-tzu, the social discipline of Confucius, and the concern with personal enlightenment of the Buddha. In the twentieth century these cultural origins branched in different directions, giving rise to the orthodox culture of Mao's Yanan, the pragmatic culture of Hong Kong's Kong-Tai, and the mix of naturalism, Confucianism, and Buddhism that characterizes the culture of contemporary Japan. The Kong-Tai and Japanese branches of the Chinese cultural tradition maintained a penchant for all things concrete and practical, and it is not surprising that the societies where it held sway managed to adopt, and even improve on, Western technology. But, though these Eastern cultures became "modernized," they did not become Westernized. Their own brand of modernism remained culturally specific—the very reason why, to this day, Japanese work habits and group loyalties cannot be transplanted in Europe and America.

The scientific-technological culture that evolved in Europe and the United States has its own characteristics. Although it tends to dismiss the perceptions of traditional peoples as the fantasies of a pre-scientific mode of thinking, the modern scientific mentality also populates the world with unseen forces and entities. These forces and entities are not, of course, supernatural forces and spirits, but scientific "constructs": entities such as quarks and photons, electromagnetic and nuclear forces, and the 200-odd particles that make up what physicists whimsically refer to as "the elementary particle zoo."

Westerners typically believe that the constructs of science are real, whereas the spirits and forces of traditional cultures are not. Yet it is wrong to attribute dogmatic certainty to any pronouncement that science might make about the real world. Scientific theories, as philosopher Karl Popper pointed out, are always *improvable,* but they are never *provable.* Openness to disconfirmation and falsification are essential hallmarks of the contemporary scientific enterprise. They should be hallmarks also of the worldview based on that enterprise.

Western science gave birth to modern technology, but the uses and benefits of technology are not limited to Western societies. The Japanese and East Asian examples show that there are many ways of applying, even of creating, technology. The new technologies do not serve exclusively their own cultural progenitors. Microelectronics, laser, robotics, bio- and genetic-engineering, artificial intelligence, new materials, waste management, information management, and system control are developed and employed by different people, in different cultural contexts.

Cultural adaptability is especially true of the technologies of information and communication: They can serve all peoples and cultures. That Western people employ information and communication to pursue socioeconomic goals of a quantitative and materialist kind does not mean that in other societies such systems would not be capable of promoting different aspirations, inspired by different values and perceptions. The artificial nervous system that is now emerging in human society is as universal as the human brain and nervous system.

Whether one shares the Western scientific-technological culture, the transcendentalist Latin culture, the animist culture of Africa, or the great cultural traditions of the Arab world and the Orient, one would be guilty of the sin of dogmatism to believe that only his or her own culture is ultimately true. It is wiser, and far more desirable, to recognize the equal validity of the fundamental premises that inspire different cultural views and values. Doing so makes possible intercultural understanding and respect, which are the basic preconditions of peace and survival on our multicultural planet.

THE CULTURE OF INTEREXISTENCE

Learning to live together is not simply a moral imperative; it is our only chance of survival.
FEDERICO MAYOR, UNESCO DIRECTOR-GENERAL

Cultural differences, if not perceived as mutually complementary, can be a dangerous thing. Many conflicts that seem economic or political on the surface harbor deep-seated cultural intolerance. For example, the fundamentalism of some elements

of the Islamic world; the conflict between Catholics and Protestants in Ireland; the civil war in Sri Lanka; the tensions between India and Pakistan; the rifts in China regarding Tibet;
the "violencia" in Latin America with its "Shining Path"; the
conflicts south of the Sahara, whether in Somalia, the Horn of
Africa, Mozambique, Angola, or Liberia; and the persistent
upheavals that rock the former Soviet Union and Yugoslavia.
Though often overlooked, internecine conflict in our time is
not merely or even primarily a matter of politics or economics: It is a cultural matter, with deep roots in historically
evolved values and perceptions.

If we are to understand and respect cultural differences
and make use of them for assuring our survival and development, we must do more than just tolerate them. Letting people
be what they want "as long as they stay in their corner of the
world," and letting them *do* what they want "as long as they
don't do it in my backyard" are well-meaning but inadequate
attitudes. In the last decade of the twentieth century, different
people and different societies must do more than merely tolerate one another; They must learn to complete and complement
one another.

If cultural differences are to be actually valued, we should
look again at a concept that appears to have been thrown on
the dustheaps of history. This concept is *coexistence.*

Coexistence originated between World Wars I and II,
when a Soviet harvest failure made outside help imperative
and the United States agreed to cover the shortfall from its agricultural surplus. Later, when both the United States and the
U.S.S.R. developed nuclear arsenals and realized that an all-out
confrontation between them would be suicidal for all parties,
the concept gained wide currency. The doctrine of coexistence
did not do away with mutual mistrust and animosity, but it did
put a lid on the actions that would follow from it. This made it
possible for the war of propaganda and the politics of power
to continue without incurring the risk of a nuclear showdown.

In the course of time, the two superpowers perceived more

and more areas of mutually beneficial collaboration. Besides agricultural trade, these areas included space technology and scientific and cultural exchange. The advantages of joining forces in selected areas outweighed the perceived benefits of economic competition and ideological confrontation. The politics of propaganda and saber rattling were played down, and detente became the key word. A quarter of a century after the end of World War, the cold war began to wind down.

The 1980s introduced glasnost into the Soviet Union and Eastern Europe, and by the end of that decade the disappearance of the Eastern pole of the bipolar world did away with the cold war altogether. Coexistence and detente lost all realistic significance. As Eastern Europe divested itself from Communist domination and joined the West, and as the Soviet Union outlawed its Communist Party and then disaggregated to independent states, the question became not how to confront the threat from the Communist world, but how to help its survivors achieve a reasonably stable and self-sufficient economic and social system.

At first, pragmatic politicians and business leaders believed that a free market primed with some capital would be a panacea. This, however, turned out to be an illusion. Though for the most part the Russian and other formerly Soviet people rejected the Communist system, the attitudes and structures catalyzed by more than seventy years of one-party rule could be neither wiped out nor ignored—as recent elections in Eastern Europe confirm. To become effective, assistance from Western democracies will have to respect these divergences. At the same time, there is no concept even remotely as transparent and effective as coexistence to describe the new East-West relations.

Such a concept can be found. We need to replace the prefix "co" with the more timely "inter." We then get "interexistence," which denotes an active, mutually constitutive relationship, instead of a passive, purely external one. It means that individuals, societies, enterprises, and entire cultures exist not merely side by side, but *with* and *through* one another. This concept is relevant not only to East-West relations, but also to the late twentieth-century world as a whole.

There always has been interexistence within individual families, and even within particular tribes or social groups: Even in hunting and gathering societies, life was mutually dependent and based on reciprocity. But relations *between* tribes have seldom been based on such dependence. Outsiders were either immaterial to a group's existence (and if so, the tribe was mostly indifferent to them) or they were actually a threat to it, in which case the tribe tended to respond with hostility. It was only when agriculture and pastoralism were introduced and people came to live in settled communities that neighboring tribes joined together and formed villages. Later the villages became integrated into more embracing social and political systems, some of which, like the archaic empires of Babylonia and Egypt and the classical empires of India, Persia, and China, survived for millennia. In the course of time people practiced interexistence also within the city-states of Greece, the empires of Rome, and the kingdoms and princedoms of medieval Europe. But never did interexistence encompass all societies existing at a given time. Even Pax Romana, which at its time brought together the peoples of the known world, was based more on the power of Rome than on the mutual dependence of its various peoples.

We are now living at a time when there are no longer any communities or states that can dominate all other states, or even get along without some of the others. Each community, each state has become dependent on other states and communities for its economic, ecologic, and even for its territorial security. It has thus become essential that relations between communities and states be informed by the culture of internal, mutually constitutive relationships.

The culture of interexistence has an inclusive logic: It is you *and* I, they *and* we. It replaces the logic of egotism and exclusion, which says me *or* you, we *or* they. The new logic can enable people and societies to play "positive sum" win-win games. As long as the players see one another's interests as merely offsetting each other, they will engage in zero-sum games—the win of one will be the loss of the other, so that the sum of the wins and losses equals zero. But when the players perceive that their existence is interdependent and their interests coincide, they will find games in which the win of one is also the win of the other.

There are many win-win games: The principal ones are peace, economic development, and a healthy environment. The way to play these games is to do away with nuclear, biological, chemical, and the more deadly varieties of conventional weapons and create a joint peacekeeping system; to have fewer children in rapidly growing high-fertility populations; to share useful skills, technologies, and capital with poorer or less developed partners; to channel investment to education, communication, and human resource development, as well as to the building of basic economic and social infrastructures; and to respect the balances and thresholds that are vital to the integrity of nature and thus to the future of humanity. In all these games the win of one is also the win of all others; while there may be short-term sacrifices, the long-term benefits coincide.

In the last few years Europe has been learning the logic of interexistence. Despite squabbles about community rules and standards, and reluctance to ratify the Maastricht Treaty leading to closer economic and monetary union, the European Community is gradually replacing the logic of coexistence with the logic of interexistence. Not only do states historically as unfriendly as Germany and France now refrain from attacking each other, and not only do they allow each to develop its own defense force, they have even created a joint army, open to other Community members. Not only do states historically as competitive as England, Germany, Holland, and France permit one another's economies to grow without hindrances, they now form a common market with shared policies and soon with a shared currency. In regard to spheres as diverse as the economy, finance, the protection of the environment, technology development, and national defense, the member states of the Community are growing, hesitantly but progressively, into an era of interexistence.

Regrettably, in the international community as a whole the logic of interexistence has begun to be applied only in limited domains, such as humanitarian relief, peace and security, and, more recently, the environment. This situation needs to be rectified. If humanity is to survive into the next century, global partnerships will have to be forged in many more areas; the culture of interexistence will have to inform many more domains of decision-making and action.

The great advantage of the culture of interexistence is that, with its inclusive logic, it could harmonize the current forms and facets of diversity. Interexistence could become the basis for perceiving complementarity between different peoples and societies, and for creating relations of mutual benefit and support. Like the diverse organs in a body, diverse peoples and cultures could work together to maintain the whole system in which they are a part, a system that is the human community in its planetary abode.

To maintain the system of which we are a part is indeed in our best interest. This is precisely why the concept of interexistence is meaningful. *Inter* is Latin for "among" or "between" and *esse* means "to be" or "to exist." Put them together and you get *"interesse"*—the root of the modern word "interest."

Here we can and must go back to our roots. We must allow the culture of interexistence to define our interest—our best interest, in a diverse and interdependent world.

6

Catalyzing
Social Creativity

Seizing the opportunities of the grand transition while averting the dangers of the fifth wave calls for fostering the growth of creativity in all of us. This must be a high level of creativity that does not remain paralyzed when faced with unusual or unexpected problems, but can deal with them openly and flexibly. In our age of transition, cultivating such creativity in many people is a basic condition of finding our way toward an information-based global society and reaping the benefits it could confer on individuals, enterprises, states, and the whole family of peoples and nations.

Creativity is not a genetic but a cultural endowment of our species. Our genes tell us how we can survive under conditions that have reigned for millions of years. But genes change slowly: Only one-half of 1 percent of our genetic endowment is likely to change in an entire century. Clearly, we no longer live in the natural jungle of the wild; we live in the artificial jungle of modern civilization. This environment we have created ourselves, and only we can cope with it. We must learn to do so. We have the capability in principle: It is the culture-based ability to code and re-code our ways of thinking and acting, time and time again.

While we *can* do this, whether or not we will actually do it is not certain. The task is not simple. It calls for drawing on the deepest and most potent sources of social creativity that are at our disposal: science, art, religion, and education.

THE ROLE OF SCIENCE

In catalyzing creativity in contemporary people, the input of science is imperative. Science can shed light on many of the problems that beset humanity, from questions of ecologic balance to issues of health and well-being. The grand transition itself is an evolutionary phenomenon capable of scientific investigation, and so are the shocks and bifurcations that beset its path. Scientists need to discuss the new knowledge emerging from their work with the widest public, outlining the problems and clarifying the options for coping with them. Since both the problems and the feasible ways of handling them require a global overview, the injection of scientific information into the debates on current issues is bound to promote the development of a kind of creativity that extends to the whole of the human community and its planetary environment.

Science can become a potent source of creativity in today's world only if scientists do not take refuge in the classical ideal of a neutral and disinterested science, aloof from what Galileo called "the passions that divide men." Scientists must recognize their close ties with society and become committed to creating the public awareness that is capable of recognizing these problems and framing effective solutions to them. Many of them do already, as the growing number of activist organizations testify, from concerned physicists and geneticists to ecologists and medical scientists.

THE ROLE OF ART

Art, like science, could be an important factor in the growth of social creativity. Art is creativity par excellence, and it is not limited to museums, galleries, and concert halls but is omnipresent in society. It shapes cities through architecture and urban design; penetrates the heart through music; entertains, challenges, and informs through literature, theater, film, and television. Though seldom recognized, our ways of thinking and acting are deeply shaped by the "pure" as well as by the "applied" arts.

Unfortunately, contemporary artists often divorce themselves from social concerns. Many painters, sculptors, musicians, and poets turn inward, in search of laws and meanings that they believe to be specific to their art. Some composers act as if Schönberg's dictum were true: If a work is art, it is not for all; and if it is for all, it is not art. This posture deprives society of an important source of creativity. Art leads to fresh insights into the human condition, giving birth to new values and ideals. Artists can teach us to see, to hear, and to come to terms with the grand transition in which we live. The performing arts are especially potent sources of social creativity. They cannot only galvanize adoration and trigger controversy, they can also trigger novel ways of seeing and innovative ways of thinking about the world.

If artists would let the dangers and opportunities we confront at this critical juncture in history inspire their artistic creativity, they could inspire our own creativity in turn. We would come to better comprehend the challenges of the grand transition, and find the values and the behaviors through which we could avoid its pitfalls and make use of its opportunities. This, indeed, is the proposition to which the newly founded "Budapest Club" is dedicated. Chaired by this writer, the Budapest Club is modeled after the internationally renowned think tank The Club of Rome, with which it is associated. It is to enlist one hundred top-level artists and writers in its membership. Its objective is to translate rational insights into the problems of our epoch into spontaneously meaningful aesthetic experiences.

THE ROLE OF RELIGION

Religion is also a critical factor in creating a new level of social creativity. There is more to our rational and emotional needs than scientific reason and aesthetic experience alone can satisfy. We also require meaning and a connection to something greater than us, even that sense of the sacred that is so highly valued in traditional societies. Religion can respond to these needs. It does not become superfluous even when science and art are tuned to human concerns. Science, after all, does not address the issues of ultimate meaning and truth, not to mention divine will and purpose. And art, while it does occasionally take up themes and issues of transcendental significance, treats them mainly in an aesthetic and intuitive manner.

We may not adhere to any doctrine or visit any church, temple, or synagogue, yet we are likely to be influenced by Christian, Jewish, Moslem, Hindu, Buddhist, Taoist, Confucian, or other values and perspectives. The insights and intuitions of the world's religions are crucial for orienting our creativity so that we may find a positive path of development. It is unfortunate that the ecumenism and humanism of many religions is overshadowed by parochial concerns. Competition between particular faiths offering a path to fulfillment and salvation in exclusive possession of the truth displaces affirmations of universal oneness and harmony.

Ever since Communism has disappeared as a world power, the politics of faith transformed from a common cause against an oppressor to a source of division among the liberated. Ethnic passions have risen from the ashes of the cold war. Religion has become one of the markers that delineates the battle lines that reach from Bosnia-Herzegovina to Serbia, from Azerbaijan to Armenia, from Pakistan to India, and from Iraq and Iran to Kuwait, Saudi Arabia, Egypt, and Israel. Again and again, Moslems and Jews, Buddhists and Hindus, Catholics and Protestants wage holy wars and shed the blood of imagined or real adversaries—and innocent bystanders.

If the great religions were to live up to their potential as catalysts of social creativity, they would also have to live up to the original meaning of their name, which is *religare:* to bind together. On our increasingly crowded and vulnerable planet, the ties among people of different races and creeds cannot be dogmatic; they must be fresh and creative. As ecumenical organizations, such as the World Council of Churches and a growing number of spiritual nongovernmental organizations recognize, the great religions could point the way to the deeper sources from which uncoercive and undogmatic ties of lasting value could spring forth, giving substance to the oneness that is the precondition of life in a globalized environment.

THE ROLE OF EDUCATION

Even if science, art, and religion influence our thinking and feeling, we are not all directly reached by these great cultural forces. The creativity inherent in science, art, and religion must move beyond the confines of studies, laboratories, studios, and places of worship, to the centers of learning in society.

The contemporary educational system should become a place of social creativity. This is seldom the case today. Our schools convey a system of knowledge that is outdated and fragmented. They resist innovation and handle information as if it could be segmented along the fault lines of the natural-scientific-technical, the social-scientific-political, and the artistic-spiritual-religious subcultures. These divisions, like those between the hard sciences and the humanities, are now obsolete and even dangerous. They prevent people from acquiring evolutionary literacy, an integrated vision of humanity in a global perspective.

A reform of the educational system in the domain of the social sciences is of particular urgency. Social and civic study programs in almost every part of the world foster what boards of education euphemistically call the "national ethos," which in reality is the root of ethnocentrism, narrow ingroup loyalties, and outright chauvinism in adults. Such programs fail on the score of flexibility and creativity; they are at best status-quo oriented and at worst an active source of international and intercultural intolerance. As children grow up, such categorizations become internalized as part of their personality. They are expressed in attitudes that influence social and political processes in their own countries and, through public opinion and political process, in the rest of our interdependent world.

It is now imperative that the schools of the former communist world stop inculcating outmoded ideologies. (For the most part, they are busy rewriting their school texts.) It is also important that Western-style democracies cease promulgating the narrow and shortsighted ethos that often accompanies expositions of "the philosophy of the free world."

If schools are to become cradles of social creativity, basic textbooks need to be rethought and rewritten. Recent reviews of the textbooks used in civics and social studies courses in U.S. and European schools show that the usual emphasis is on national history rather than the history of others; that events and episodes from one's own history are presented in a manner that encourages children to believe that their land is superior to all others; and that when other countries are discussed they appear either as friends or enemies, not in terms of their own culture and achievements. Most school texts do not call for debate and critical thinking, only for acceptance. Primary and secondary teachers seldom spur debate; they do not like to deal with political controversy. Their role, they mostly believe, is to help children become loyal citizens with due respect for, and obedience to, public and institutional authority.

Despite their undoubted achievements in the transmission of specialized learning, our educational systems sadly lack creative drive. They typically promote conformity, passivity, and parochial sentiments. This state of affairs is just as obsolete as the segmentation of the knowledge system itself. There is an urgent need for educational programs that lead to discovery and do not stop at instruction; that encourage insight, not merely the accumulation of information; and that foster personal involvement rather than passive emulation. There is a parallel need for teachers who can raise and help formulate questions rather than prescribe answers, who dare to challenge values and assumptions rather than bolster established conceptions.

The fostering of social creativity is a major challenge to our schools and colleges. If they do not muster the will and the determination to revise outdated beliefs, update obsolete images, and correct misguided practices, there is not much chance that the public will develop the creativity required of every man, woman, and child in this age of rapid change and boundless threat as well as opportunity.

As sources of social creativity, science, art, religion, and education have a major role and responsibility in today's world. This role does not demean scientists, artists, educators, and men and women of faith by putting their own insights and creativity at the service of preconceived ends; on the contrary, it lends concrete value to them. Through their creative efforts we could come to see the grand transition in which we live in fresh perspectives.

- From the perspective of science, we would see the transition as the lawlike evolution of a complex system through a developmental dynamic that is irreversible, though it is nonlinear and full of shocks and surprises.

- From the perspective of art, the transition would be an adventure replete with drama and significance, bringing to us new insights to guide our steps in interpersonal and intercultural relationships.

- And from the viewpoint of religion, the transition would appear endowed with transcendental meaning and significance, a testament to the continuing advance of humankind toward a higher and more divine unity.

Catalyzing creativity in today's world deserves a collective effort equal to the great national projects of the past. But this effort, unlike the Manhattan Project, which created the atomic bomb that ended World War II, or the Apollo Mission that first put men on the moon, has neither a military nor a space objective. Its objective is humanistic and universal: to catalyze the capability in contemporary people to creatively confront the problems all of us now face in common.

III

THE IMPERATIVES
OF ACTION

7

The Citizens' Guide to Life on a Small Planet

It is time to move from the realm of perception to the sphere of action. Action begins at home with what we do in our daily life, you and I, and thousands and millions like us. Let us pose, then, the following question: What can I do, a concerned citizen who is neither particularly influential nor particularly powerful, to improve the odds that the human family—and my own family—will survive and prosper in the twenty-first century?

There are three basic rules of thumb that we can follow to improve the odds.

THE FIRST RULE: THINK GLOBALLY

Thinking in ways that are adapted to our crucial epoch is a uniquely human capacity. Humanity has now become dependent on its proper exercise. Animals can learn by experience, but their basic behavior remains guided by instinct, and instinct cannot be changed, except by the slow processes of mutation and natural selection. We humans, however, can learn by experience, and our conscious thinking can transcend our inherited instincts.

The dominance of instinct by experience makes for a swift process: It is what distinguishes the single-generational cultural evolution of people from the many-generational genetic evolution of animals. Yet reliance on the experience of one or a few generations also can wreak havoc, and under changing circumstances it even can become a threat to survival. Unlike basic instincts, which are bound to be functional (had they not been, they would have been eliminated by natural selection), behaviors selected in the light of experience also can be faulty. The action patterns and lifestyles that emerge in the time and place of one generation can turn obsolete in the time and place of the next.

The risk of making wrong choices of behavior and lifestyle is, of course, only one side of the coin; the other is the chance to make right ones. Making right choices calls for a sound appreciation of the facts and factors that govern our existence. Global thinking contributes to this task: It enables us to see the forest, not just the trees. But the promise of global thinking is not to produce universal blueprints for right choices in all circumstances; instead, it is to bring to us the perspective in which we can make right choices of our own.

Today, global thinking has become the necessary framework for effective and responsible living and acting. This does not mean thinking in vague and general categories, or in millions and billions, whether of human beings or barrels of oil. It is thinking in terms of processes, not of structures; in terms of dynamic wholes, not of static parts. Global thinking is not a simplistic, one-dimensional way of thinking. It takes note of the complexity of this world but is not overawed by it. It perceives the potential for achieving unity in the womb of diversity, and harmony in the web of complexity.

Global thinking leaves behind the mechanistic and simplistic belief that one can fix what is wrong like fixing a broken bicycle: by replacing the malfunctioning part. Society, after all, is not a man-made mechanism where mechanics can fix poorly functioning people and obsolete institutions by using ready-made tools and following preconceived instructions. Rather, each individual must start with himself or herself to guide the dynamic of social change toward desired, and responsibly desirable, outcomes.

Globally thinking persons can become effective and responsible agents of social change. Not only do they perceive that this world is a tightly interconnected and interdependent system that transits from one phase of development into another, they also comprehend the essential logic of its development, the nature of its complex yet ordered dynamics. They know that nature and society do not evolve from one point of time to another and then cease. Change is continuous, complete stability an illusion. The best people can do is to guide the evolutionary process so as to avoid unpleasant shocks and untenable conditions. But such guidance is possible, and it does not come from outside and above, but from inside and below. Globally thinking persons give up looking to leaders and larger-than-life heroes to take matters into hand; they recognize their own role in the evolutionary transition.

Guiding desirable social change through participation is what "empowerment" is all about. Empowered individuals recognize that they have the power to change themselves and their environment, but divest themselves of the adolescent belief that they can rule and master the world around them. They know that human control is real but indirect and that, in consequence, the insight one brings to the process must be sound. It is competence that globally thinking persons are after, not omnipotence.

THE SECOND RULE: ACT MORALLY

Competence is essential, but it is not everything. Sound insight must be complemented by sound principles in applying it. This is where moral considerations come in.

Moral action in the contemporary world rests on a simple and meaningful principle, a crucial variant on the laissez-faire concept of "live and let live." Today, the principle of morality is not just to live and let others live as they please, but to *live in a way that allows other people to live as well*. Remarkably enough, this principle was formulated by philosopher Immanuel Kant in the eighteenth century. His celebrated "categorical imperative" states that a person's action should be capable of becoming a universal maxim: that is, everyone should be able to act the same way. This is not just "live and let live," nor is it "do unto others as you would have others do unto you." Rather, it is to do to others, to ourselves, and to society and nature, what others could also do without destroying themselves, us, society, and nature.

At a time when everyone is becoming interdependent, and when ever more people demand a fair slice of a no-longer growing pie, acting in a way that could be repeated by all people without inducing chaos and catastrophe is imperative. When all is said and done, it is the only way we can be sure of averting a slide from interdependence into polarization—and then into violence and chaos.

In this day and age acting in accordance with the categorical imperative, though essential, is far from easy: It calls for considerable changes in the way most people actually act. The relatively privileged strata of society still live in a way that the less

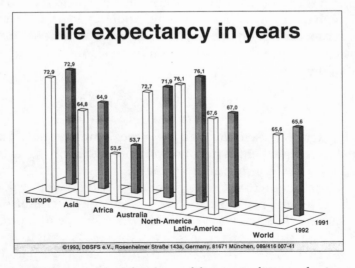

Differences in the lifestyles and living conditions of privileged and underprivileged populations are reflected in different average life expectations (here pictured by continent).

privileged strata could not duplicate. The planet has neither the resources nor the carrying capacity for all people to drive private cars, live in separate homes, and use the myriad gadgets and appliances that go with the typical lifestyle of the affluent.

Changes are also called for on the part of the less privileged populations: They, in turn, must cease to emulate the lifestyles of the affluent. It would not be enough for Americans to reduce harmful emissions and economize on energy if the Chinese continue to burn coal for electricity and wood for cooking, and acquire Western driving habits.

All people everywhere must do their best not to rob others of the chance to live their own lives. They must learn not to deplete nonrenewable resources, overuse renewable ones, or stretch the tolerance thresholds of nature's regenerative cycles. All people must accept that you and I, and not just "the others," must change our dominant values and habitual ways. Change is not the privilege of the powerful, nor the constraint of the powerless, but the moral responsibility of everyone.

Changing our values and actions so as to be in harmony with the categorical imperative has concrete and practical implications. Consider, for example, the matter of family size. People in most industrialized societies realize that there is no need to have more children than they can properly care for and educate. But this realization has not penetrated to millions, indeed billions, in the poorer parts of the world. Underprivileged couples in traditional societies often believe that they should have as many children as God, or good fortune, allows them to have. They hold that having many children speaks well of virility in men and femininity in women. And they also believe (alas, sometimes not without reason) that they need many children, especially boys, to take care of them in old age. These beliefs make for more children than they can support and educate. Often, they make for more children than the couples themselves would wish. Many people in poor and traditional regions of the world are not familiar with birth control techniques for limiting their offspring or spacing their births as they would wish.

Failing to limit one's family size according to actual need makes for immoral behavior. It comes up against the rule "live in a way that allows others to live as well." If we all had as many children as we wanted, the next generation could not have *any* children, or would have to face the fact that the children it brought into the world could not be adequately cared for and may never grow into healthy adults.

Then there is the question of consumption. Everybody knows that modern industrial societies are consumer societies, where if not the consumer, then certainly consumption, is king. But not everybody knows that unrestrained consumption is downright immoral: It wastes so many precious resources and is so harmful to the environment that it could not be indulged in by anyone but a privileged minority.

Environmentalists say that the only thing to do is to consume as little as possible—there are no *good* ways to consume. Clearly, however, there are responsible and irresponsible ways. Ever more of the products offered in modern societies are recycled or recyclable, biodegradable, sparing of nonrenewable materials and energies, and environmentally friendly in use and manufacture. Increasingly, we are offered solutions that are permanent or at least long-lasting, and energy- and raw-materials efficient. A truly responsible consumer buys and uses products that can be recycled or reused, last longer, and are not harmful to nature whether in use, disposal, or manufacture. Whenever possible, such a consumer substitutes services for products and makes use of lasting solutions, such as insulation, instead of opting for ongoing consumption—such as keeping on the furnace or the air conditioner.

Our eating habits, too, need to be thought about: They are part of our behavior pattern and can be moral or immoral, much as any other lifestyle choice. While we must eat, what we eat is up to us—and there are responsible and irresponsible ways of choosing our daily food. The responsible way is more important than most people realize: What we eat has much to do with what others eat, and even whether they eat at all. Poor eating habits rob vast populations of the chance to obtain food of their own.

Morality in eating concerns first of all the amount of meat we eat. It is becoming increasingly immoral to produce grain only to feed it to animals that are slaughtered for their meat. The great majority of the human population would be unable to follow the kind of diet that is still dominant in industrialized countries: All the produce of the six continents would not be sufficient to meet that level of meat consumption. This is not because we could not breed enough pigs and cows, but because we could not grow enough grain to feed the pigs and cows. Feeding grain to domestic animals wastes most of it: They must live and grow in their own right, and for that they need caloric energy. They get it from the grain and other feedstuff provided to them; in exchange, they provide milk, eggs, and meat. But the caloric energy provided by the meat of a cow is only about one-seventh of the caloric energy consumed by the cow itself. This means that the process of converting grain into beef wastes six-sevenths (more than 85 percent) of the caloric value of the planet's primary produce. The pertinent proportion is somewhat better in poultry: The average chicken returns about one-third of the caloric value of its feedstuff in the form of meat and eggs.

The bottom line is that if everyone on the six continents ate steaks and hamburgers like the average Westerner, the world's total grain production would not suffice to feed the world's population. The giant herds of cattle and endless farms of poultry would require more grain than the total output of the world's cultivated lands, according to some calculations, twice as much. Given the amount of land available for farming and the available agricultural methods, doubling today's grain production is not feasible. This should give us pause, quite apart from the morality of slaughtering endless millions of helpless animals. But if people in industrialized countries would aim for grain-based food self-sufficiency, the rpesent level of agricultural production would be enough to feed all people in the world, far into the future.

Eating in a way that everyone can eat does not require us to go hungry, or even to deprive ourselves of plentiful healthy food. It means only eating more directly what our lands produce.

Happily, a caloric-energy-efficient diet is not only more moral, it is also *healthier* than a wasteful one. When our fathers and grandfathers spent the day in heavy manual work in fields or factories, they could come home to eat a hearty meat dish. Their bodies needed the extra calories and could get rid of the extra fat. But people in modern societies have a mainly sedentary lifestyle, with physical exercise limited to running to catch commuter trains. Consequently they require food of high nutritional value in an easily digestible form. As nutritionists are discovering, vegetables, fruit, cereals, and fresh produce in general fit the bill; red meat, high in fat and cholesterol, does not.

Many people do not switch to more adapted diets in greater numbers because of the persistence of obsolete values and beliefs. For some men the ability to tuck away a large T-bone steak is still a mark of virility; and for some women being able to afford high-grade meat is still a source of satisfaction, while "having to do without" is an admission of having failed to keep up with the Joneses.

What goes for meat eating goes for many prepared and luxury foods as well. Prepared foods create convenience and save time, but they also make for more waste. More energy goes into preparing a meal, and more materials are involved in getting it on the table. A brown paper bag to carry a pound of fresh groceries accounts for only 0.6 percent of the food's weight, but when the same groceries are canned, the container makes up 13.5 percent of its weight. And if the same food is film-wrapped for microwave cooking, the packaging comes to over 16 percent. The extra packaging not only wastes raw material; it also inflates the stream of solid waste going from households to expensive and scarce disposal facilities.

Indulging some habits, such as smoking, has unsuspectedly wide consequences. That cigarettes use paper to hold the tobacco and that they require paper for packaging is obvious, and that smoking would be dangerous to one's health can be read on every package. But that the use of tobacco is unfair to untold millions of the world's poor is not generally known. The land on which most poor country farmers grow tobacco for export could be used to grow grain and vegetables to feed the local hungry. But as long as there is a market for it, farmers will plant tobacco instead of wheat, corn, or soya. And there will be a market for tobacco as long as there is a demand for cigarettes and cigars among the well-to-do (and even the not-so-well-to-do) people of this world.

Tobacco, together with other "cash crops" such as coffee and tea, commands a considerable portion of the planet's fertile lands, yet no cash crop is a real life necessity. Reducing the demand for such items as coffee and tobacco would mean a healthier life for the rich, and a chance for adequate nourishment for the poor. While abstaining from a heavy diet of meat and overcoming a dependence on tobacco, coffee, and other stimulants would not automatically put more food on the tables of the hungry, it would make it possible for the world's agricultural lands to feed the entire human population—a basic consideration when it comes to assuring the long-term conditions for sustaining life on a small and crowded planet.

The use of the automobile is yet another case in point. The automotive use–patterns that evolved in the industrialized countries could not be duplicated in the nonindustrialized ones: The world would run out of oil and breathable air in a matter of years.

On the other hand, in the industrialized countries the car is not only used, it is overused. As the bulk of the cost is in the initial purchase of a car and not in its use, there is little incentive for people to reduce their driving habits. Some drive so much that they need to go to health spas to exercise on walking machines. Ownership has become a matter of psychological gratification, and the choice of make and model a matter of prestige. Driving habits often respond to the need to vent aggressiveness, rather than to fill a need for transportation.

The unreflective spread of private-car-based shopping centers and industrial and service areas has made for urban sprawls that eat some of the world's most productive farmlands. In the U.S., the land covered by metropolitan areas has doubled in the last thirty years, with streets, parking lots, and buildings that replace oxygen-producing vegetation with concrete surfaces that require much energy to build, further energy to light and maintain, and additional energy and materials to move people to and from their places of residence. With the overuse of cars, modern cities are spreading over rural surroundings, city centers are depopulating, neighborhood businesses are dying, and neighborhoods are becoming dehumanized. Many city blocks are little more than a collection of houses with streets that people use to drive away from to satisfy their daily needs.

A globally thinking and morally acting person would think twice before taking a car to town when public transport is available. Even when using an efficient gasoline-powered vehicle, running thirty-four miles to the gallon and using a catalytic converter, a commuter doing 15,000 miles a year emits close to 5 tons of CO_2 into the air. This is almost three times the 1.7 tons that the UN's Panel on Climate Change believes is the upper limit of per-person CO_2 production without serious risk of global warming. However, using public transport for going to work and shopping and limiting the use of a diesel-powered private vehicle to necessary trips and leisure-time activities would bring one's share of annual CO_2 production well below 2 tons. And if commuter trains, buses, and subways were kept clean and well running, traveling on them in company with others could be more pleasant than fighting traffic on the highway in the isolation of the private car, not to mention sitting blocked in a traffic jam.

Daily drivers are not naive: They realize that using their own cars in city traffic is becoming less and less pleasant, efficient, and economical. In bigger cities an increasing number of them consider the consequences of traffic as nearly unbearable. In Europe, for example, this was the view of 39 percent of drivers in Vienna, 37 percent in Frankfurt, and 34 percent in Hannover. In cities large and small drivers are becoming open to the idea that they should shift to public transport, more of them, in fact, than politicians and public-opinion experts give credit for.

In a recent poll in Holland, 60 percent of Dutch drivers said that they thought it possible to switch from the use of private cars to public transport on a voluntary basis, whereas public-opinion experts estimated that only 14 percent would think so, and 86 percent would believe that such a shift would call for some form of coercion. On the other hand, drivers often hold mistaken views of the advantages of car travel as opposed to travel by public means. On a scale in which 100 indicated the actual cost of a trip, drivers in Germany placed the cost of their private automobile at 55 and that of city transport at 113. They also held mistaken views regarding how long such trips would take. Compared to a factual average time indicated by 100, they thought they could complete a trip by their own car at 85 percent of this time, whereas they put the time required to complete it by public means at 132.

Surveys have shown that it is not enough to build on the willingness of the drivers alone. The members of their family would have to follow suit as well. In the German city of Stuttgart a public information campaign asked motorists to make an experiment: Use city transport to go to work for a period of one month. The number of drivers polled in that period raised the use of city buses and trams by 81 percent, but the total gain for public transport came to only 5 percent. It turned out that family members left their habitual buses and trams in favor of the family car conveniently left at home.

We can and must make rational choices even in regard to such emotional issues as the use of the family automobile. Responsible use means only such use as cannot be efficiently and economically replaced by public transport, or by bicycling and walking.

Acting morally does not call for sacrificing our health, or even our standard of living. There is often a coincidence between obeying the categorical imperative and living the good life. Riding a bike or traveling by subway or bus, insulating the home so that we can cut down on the use of heating fuel, using fluorescent rather than the more energy-intensive incandescent bulbs, and reusing, repairing, and recycling whatever we buy and consume are not less pleasant or less effective in regard to satisfying our material needs than making use of wasteful technologies, products, and practices. Taking responsibility for our society and our environment meshes well with taking care of ourselves: The efficient alternative is usually also the one that is happier and healthier.

The moral side of lifestyle choices is just as important as the rational side. We should do the right thing not only because it is the most efficient and rational thing to do, but also because we know, even *feel,* that it is the right one. A moral individual finds waste and pollution not only inefficient; he or she finds it intrinsically unacceptable. In such a person a plastic bag thrown out of a speeding car or a smokestack belching carbon dioxide evokes repugnance and something akin to physical pain, independently of the dollars-and-cents reasoning underlying the economics of pollution control and the cleanup of solid waste and atmospheric emission.

For morally acting persons all things acquire the vivid colors of ethical relevance; few if any remain gray and neutral. Endowed with the colors of right and wrong, desirable and undesirable, moral and immoral, the world of globally thinking and morally acting individuals becomes a well-marked playing field, conducive to purposeful action.

THE THIRD RULE: LIVE RESPONSIBLY

I believe that every individual has a responsibility to help guide our global family in the right direction. . . . I, for one, really do believe that individuals can make a difference in society. Because periods of great change, such as the pres-

*ent, come so rarely in human history, it is up to each of us
to use our time well for the creation of a happier world.*
TENZIN GYATSO, THE XIVTH DALAI LAMA

The third rule is to accept multiple spheres of responsibility. These include the private sphere of the individual, the political sphere of the citizen, as well as the economic sphere of the blue- and the white-collar worker.

Accepting multiple spheres of responsibility means making considered choices in every domain of life and existence.

- What work or profession do we choose: something by which to amass the most money in the shortest time, or an activity that is meaningful in itself and beneficial to others?

- What technologies do we make use of in the enterprise: wasteful and polluting ones as long as they manage to squeeze out a high rate of profit, or resource-efficient ones that respect nature and community?

- How do we furnish our home: with synthetic ostentation, or for coziness, health, and sociability?

- What materials do we select for home and personal use: nonbiodegradable synthetics mass-produced in global chemical concerns, or natural fibers produced from plants in our own region?

- And how do we clothe ourselves and our family: for fashion or for genuine self-expression; in ways that feed our ego, or in ways that preserve our family and community values and our cultural heritage?

Responsible persons have positive personalities and healthy lifestyles. They eat, rest, and exercise rationally, engage in a diverse range of activities, and take a long-range view of the consequences of their actions. They make good leaders and conscientious team members. They are comfortable being alone but enjoy working and playing with others, and are capable of loving and respecting all people, whether of the same or of a different color, creed, or culture.

Responsible individuals know how to make moral choices, balancing actions that are immediately advantageous to themselves with those that are beneficial to their culture and their society. They are alive in every sense of the word, with a zest for living, loving, and learning, as well as for communicating and cooperating. Morally acting responsible persons are a vital force and a crucial factor in the historic transition toward a sustainable and cooperative information-based society.

If today's concerned citizen recognizes the relevant spheres of responsibility and engages in global thinking and moral action, his or her changed values and actions would spread on the turbulent, information-linked seas of the contemporary world. There are many grass-roots movements that would resonate to the emerging values and convictions—movements for natural living, for peace and nonviolence, for the protection of the environment, and for intercultural understanding, among others. There would also be civic and political leaders who would listen. Even the mass media would pick up the scent: Newspapers, radio, and TV are becoming sensitized to movements that carry new values and form new behaviors. Today, innovative ideas and actions have better-than-ever chances of getting on the air and into print.

In the fifth century B.C., Chinese sage Lao-tzu wrote in his famous *Tao-te-ching:* "One's individual life serves as an example for other individuals; one's family serves as a model for other families; one's community serves as a standard for other communities; one's state serves as a measure for other states; and one's country serves as an ideal for all countries." How do I know this? he then asked. "It is," he answered, "obvious."

If this was obvious in the geographically and culturally fragmented world of the fifth century B.C., it should be all the more obvious in the interconnected and thoroughly informated world of today. In this world thinking globally and acting morally with multiple spheres of responsibility could prove to be nationally and even globally "contagious"—not a virus in itself, but the antibody to the virus of egotism, short-sightedness, intolerance, and irresponsibility.

When all is said and done, as we head toward the twenty-first century a global perspective is the best approach to moral action, and moral action by responsible citizens is the best hope for species survival and individual well-being.

ACTION POINT: THE CPC STRATEGY

Global thinking, joined with moral action and responsible living, signifies a new and vital mutation in human consciousness. It should be developed and diffused. Doing so is essential: It would ground those values, priorities, and lifestyles that can ensure our survival.

The consciousness we need encompasses a view of the planet as a globally extended system that evolves as a seamless whole. Holism is the "forest" dimension of the new consciousness, while the analytical "trees" dimension discloses the elements that pose threats (such as overpopulation, poverty, waste and pollution, militarization, climate change, deforestation, and food and energy squeezes, among others), as well as the elements that convey opportunities. A consciousness that embraces both dimensions in a meaningful way is a "Wei-ji" consciousness—a consciousness of global crisis as a process that gives us the chance to transform our lives.

The timely development of such a consciousness is too important to be left to serendipity. Serendipity may favor us for a while, as it often does when matters of human survival are at stake, but it is not reliable. It needs to be reinforced with purposive action, aimed at intensifying the factors that help people develop a new consciousness on their own. Such action cannot be entrusted to luck, nor can it be entrusted to the ordinary mechanisms of the market. The market is a powerful instrument, but it is notoriously shortsighted. It responds to demand that exists already, and not to demand that will exist in the future, even if such demand would serve the actors' long-term interests. Myopia is built not only into trade, consumer, and capital markets, but also into educational and informational ones.

Obeying current market forces would retard the spread of the new consciousness by making a chicken-and-egg situation: The new consciousness will be produced and diffused if, but only if, there is a serious demand for it. But there will be such a demand only if the new consciousness has already captured the mind of the public, meaning that it has been already produced and diffused. Something must be done to break this self-reinforcing cycle. In normal times market mechanisms are beneficial; they distribute costs and benefits. But in times of crisis, when there is a paramount need to initiate rapid and purposive change, they can become unadapted. If they are to turn beneficial again, we must reach a condition in which demand reflects long-term need, and thus catalyzes products that are useful also in the long term.

If serendipity is to be reinforced, and the vicious cycle created by the uncontrolled mechanism of the market is to be broken, upcroppings of the new consciousness must be purposefully fostered. This calls for bringing together the right people with the right ideas, and endowing them with the right means and the right structures.

The task would be easier if today's powerful and well-endowed schools and colleges would be ready to develop and diffuse the newly emerging consciousness on their own. But with few exceptions, they are not. On the whole, the more prestigious the school, the more it reflects and inculcates the views and values of the tradition that has put it on a high pedestal. But these views and values, as we have seen, are often flawed: They are both behind the times and fragmented along disciplinary and cultural lines.

In many elite prep schools and universities, established knowledge is prized to such an extent that it blocks innovation; it restricts the inflow of new ideas. Generation after generation, departments and faculties replicate their own mind-sets.

In colleagues as well as in students, educators reward perform-ance that copies their own solidly entrenched views. It is not surprising that the most prestigious institutions produce indi-viduals who, on leaving the halls of academe, remain dedi-cated to the status quo in their private and professional lives.

It is sometimes said that the only body that is more conser-vative than a college of bishops is the board of trustees of a university. The remark, even if exaggerated, points to the need to explore other-than-mainstream avenues for developing and diffusing the new consciousness. These avenues cannot rely on the established public media either, since commercial radio, television, newspapers, and newsmagazines are part of the market and are trapped in its chicken-and-egg cycles. An effec-tive breakthrough calls for exploring other alternatives. They exist. Consider the initiative that you, the reader, could seize if you acted along the following lines:

First, become clear in your own mind of the requirement for a new consciousness, and of the nature of that conscious-ness. Then raise the need for developing and diffusing it among your circle of friends and associates. Bring together those of them who rally to the idea, regardless of their backgrounds and occupations. Ask them how certain key insights—relating to family size, consumer and lifestyle choices, the ecology, com-munity affairs, and politics—could be made more conrete and visible. You will find that making them concrete calls for fur-ther debate and discussion, while diffusing them requires ac-cess to the public media as well as to educational institutions. This should not discourage you. Neither the media nor the ed-ucational outlets need to be of the conservative mainstream. Alternative ways of communicating and learning are emerg-ing in profusion. You should review what is available and de-vise a strategy for reaching what you and your group has chosen.

Soon you will realize that a minimally formalized and opti-mally flexible operational structure becomes a real necessity. The first thing in creating such a structure is to give it an identity. Name your group so that its members as well as other people can refer to it. You might choose a name such as "Center for Plane-tary Consciousness." Assuming that you did, your group, now a recognizable "CPC," becomes available for contacting, and even for replication, by likeminded groups. This does not mean un-desirable competition; on the contrary, it offers a highly desir-able reinforcement through local and regional partnerships. A CPC network formed by grass-roots groups has far better chances to spread its message and become influential than any single CPC on its own. Consequently, unlike the continued spread of *CFC*s, which destroy a vital component of our physi-cal atmosphere, the spread of *CPC*s would build and nourish a part of our social and cultural atmosphere—one that is just as vital for our survival as clean and UV-radiation-free air.

Think now of incorporating your CPC as a nonprofit or-ganization, so that you may solicit suitable operating funds. In this connection it may be wise to bring your CPC onto the na-tional and international scene. Make it into an NGO or INGO (national or international nongovernmental organization). This will bring you in touch with a growing string of con-cerned citizen groups all over the nation, and potentially all over the world.

A sound operating structure will help you raise funds. While the initially shoestring budget of a CPC also can be raised from sympathetic local people in business and politics, further support can be best raised on a matching basis from national and international bodies, such as the NEH (National Endow-ment for the Humanities) in the United States, and UNESCO in the international field. A systematic survey of funding sources will disclose a variety of promising prospects. Given that the need for centers for new thinking is becoming more recognized, you will find that the old adage "Where there is a will, there is a way" holds true.

When you succeed in creating a realistic organizational and financial footing for your CPC, it is ready to branch out and interact with others of its kind. The more the initial ideas it champions are developed, the more their relevance will strike people both in your town and elsewhere. It will be the timeliness of the ideas, and not the diplomas (or lack of diplomas) of their promulgators that will confer the legitimacy on them that is necessary to ensure widespread attention. The visibility of your CPC will grow. The more foresighted elements of the information media, sensing a new gound swell in public opinion, will pick up some ideas and projects, and foresighted individuals in business and politics will start paying heed to them. Networking with other CPCs will have a multiplier effect.

In order to be truly effective, you will need to focus the output of the CPC with care. One focus will have to be the public at large. Output in this regard could include townhall meetings, debates, seminars, and other discussion forums, accompanied by pamphlets, press releases, and information notes for both journalists and concerned citizens. Another focus would have to be public education, accessed through some nonestablishment and innovation-sensitive channel. Here your output may involve guest lecturers and experimental courses, and survival- and development-related study curricula from grade school through continuing education.

In elaborating these plans and projects you will not need to emulate established institutions and practices. There is no real need for formal lecture courses in sheltered lecture halls; the indicated forms of learning are best fostered in the framework of informal debating and discussion groups, by learning-by-doing internships, and by individual study guided by responsible tutors. The new consciousness can be evolved collaboratively, by tackling concrete problems and attempting to apply realistic remedies to them. This calls for focusing the emerging insights, not fragmenting them.

The pitfall of fragmentation by idea-tight disciplinary compartments can be avoided. CPCs can be highly focused without turning specialized and losing their global overview. To ensure this objective, you need to insist that curricula be articulated within modules that are clearly located in the overarching global context. Modules could center on politics, business, the environment, society at large, or on more specific domains such as science or spirituality. By placing the issues within a framework that is planetary in scope and holistic in cross-section, the study of problems and solutions in the field selected by one module could interrelate with problems and solutions selected by the others.

If the CPC strategy is attempted and brought to fruition by a critical number of enterprising individuals, the new consciousness would surface in all the principal domains of interest, more or less at the same time. There would be something like a planetary political consciousness; a planetary business consciousness; a planetary ecological consciousness; a planetary social consciousness; and a planetary scientific and spiritual consciousness.

Pursuing strategies like this is vital for the future of humanity. The rapid spread of planetary consciousness is the best guarantee that we will embark on an evolutionary, rather than on a degenerative, path. Because the next level of stability on Earth can only be global in scope, it can be attained only if people think and act in globally conscious and responsible ways. CPCs and likeminded initiatives could spread those insights that could lead us toward a desirable destiny, rather than toward chaos and breakdown.

Responsible action requires that we now take things into our own hands. Our hands are far from ineffective: In times of turbulence new values and ideas can spread like wildfire. Our job is to make sure that humane and evolutionary values and ideas spread in society, rather than obsolete or inhuman kinds. The choice of the human future, after all, is ours. It can be neither ignored nor postponed. But it can, and therefore must, be informed and empowered.

8

The Priorities of Human Development

When politicians and experts address weighty issues such as the well-being of people and the sustainable development of society, they tend to speak of the objectives in terms of physical parameters and quantitative targets. In order to create a livable and sustainable environment, we need to reduce by X percent the carbon dioxide content of the atmosphere; combat soil erosion by replacing X tons of chemical fertilizers with organic manure; and combat desertification by reforesting X thousands of acres. To attain some degree of economic fairness and social justice, we must reduce poverty by investing X millions in slum clearance; provide X tons of food to hungry populations; and invest X dollars in underdeveloped infrastructures. The list could go on and on.

On occasion, individual objectives are grouped by categories. The Club of Rome, for example, in its 1991 report, *The First Global Revolution,* aggregated the main goals that must be achieved if there is to be a "world resolutique" of the "world problematique" into three "immediacies": reconversion from a military to a civil economy; coping with global warming and energy issues; and attending to the problems of development.

Whether listed individually or by category, there is something wrong with treating objectives in the usual way. Deeper reflection will show that goals such as reconversion to peace, stabilization of the climate, the promotion of development, and the many economic, ecologic, social, and political targets outlined today by a plethora of institutions and experts, though vital in their own right, are not properly viewed as the primary objectives of the world community. This is because their attainment is conditional on the achievement of a set of prior objectives that, if left out of account, would reduce all plans and projects to mere words.

The set of prior, truly fundamental objectives has to do with the values, perceptions, and aspirations of people, rather than with the processes that follow from them. Though these factors are subjective and cultural rather than objective and physical, we must not ignore them nor underestimate their import. Conscious action, after all, is preceded by perceptions and guided by values. If our perceptions are faulty, our actions will be misguided; and if our values are out of date, our priorities will fail to mesh with the world's changing realities.

Yet in most parts of the world, human power and potentials are sadly underdeveloped. Despite great technological progress and vast flows of information, many people remain uninformed and unprepared in the face of the challenges awaiting them. The way children are born and raised depresses their potential for learning and creativity; the way young people experience the struggle for material survival results in frustration and resentment. In adults this leads to a variety of compensatory, addictive, and compulsive behaviors. The result is the persistence of social and political oppression, economic warfare, cultural intolerance, crime, and disregard for the environment.

Eliminating social and economic ills calls for considerable socioeconomic development, and that is not possible without better education, information, and communication. These resources, however, are usually blocked by the absence of socioeconomic development, so that here, too, a vicious cycle is produced: Underdevelopment creates frustration, which gives rise to defective behaviors and blocks development.

This cycle must be broken at its point of greatest flexibility: the development of human resources. People must become better educated, better informed, and endowed with better communication channels. Achieving this objective does not preempt the need for socioeconomic development with all its financial and technical resources, but calls for a parallel mission in the field of culture. The problems of survival and development depend vitally on what goes on in the minds of individual people. The more a person is "developed" (not, of course, merely in the economic sense, but in the sense of being a mature and responsible citizen), the more his or her society has a chance to develop. Consequently the survival and development-related agenda of our day needs to start with the human factor: the development of the perceptions and actions of a critical mass of individuals.

THE DINOSAUR SYNDROME

Let us step back for a moment and gain a bird's-eye view of the problems of our day in reference to people's ability to perceive and assess them. We can make use of an odd-sounding but relevant biological metaphor: society as a self-maintaining and adapting "social organism."

It is beyond question that human society, like a human being, is a complex system that maintains itself in a changing and dynamic environment. Societies and individuals can survive only if their internal and external environments are matched and balanced. This calls for constant sensitivity to changes in their milieu. For example, if temperature in the environment drops, people seek the warmth of clothing and shelter; if it rises, they shed clothing and seek cooling breezes. The same kind of sensitivity occurs in regard to changes in people's ecologic, social, and cultural milieu.

The "social organism," too, is sensitive to a changing environment. As conditions in the milieu of a society change, its institutions, structures, and processes are subjected to fresh constraints and provided with fresh opportunities. If society fails to respond to the emerging dangers and opportunities, or reacts with a significant time lag, its institutions become obsolete and its practices outdated. The way it copes becomes less functional and more prone to crises.

This is just what is happening to the majority of contemporary societies. The environment in which societies operate—not just the physical, chemical, and biological, but also the economic, social, and political environment—is in rapid change. Social structures and practices fail to keep pace. As a result many societies are in danger of becoming as maladapted as the dinosaurs.

The analogy is not unreasonably farfetched: Some of these prehistoric reptiles were cold-blooded, with bodies many meters long, connected by a sluggish nervous system that operated especially slowly at low ambient temperatures. The nerves that connected legs and tails to the distant head are likely to have taken several seconds instead of a few microseconds to convey signals, even if the signals carried information that was critical for the health and survival of the giant beasts.

Since the cold-blooded dinosaurs had few natural predators, their slow nervous systems did not prevent them from surviving as a species for millions of years. But we humans are not in a similarly fortunate situation. Our environment harbors many dangers, and we need a system that brings information regarding approaching dangers to our brains quickly and without fail. We have evolved it on the organic level: Our nervous systems connect our brains with our perceptual organs. But our societies are also exposed to multiple dangers, so they, too, need a fast and reliable nervous system. That system, however, has not been sufficiently evolved.

True, we have built ultrafast communication networks, but they do not convey to societies the information they need. Consequently the reaction time of many societies tends to be long, and the responses sluggish. The majority of humanity fails to perceive the shape of the evolutionary trend in which it lives. Perceptions, values, and aspirations remain adapted to a world that no longer exists, while the world that is coming to be remains a hazy dream that comes into focus only when it produces nasty shocks.

In this situation it is not enough to produce prescriptions

and blueprints, to specify targets and advocate objectives, essential though these tasks are in themselves. As long as the main body of society fails to receive clear and urgent signals relating to its changed environment, the best thought-out plans and projects remain paper tigers, good for triggering speeches and little else. This condition endangers not only the sluggish societies but even those that would be ready to respond with more alacrity. With all societies becoming interdependent, lagging perceptions and faulty judgments in one society have negative consequences in all.

We can and should rectify this "dinosaur syndrome." Experts should not stop at producing blueprints and strategies for action, for in the absence of clear and urgent signals relating to the value of their realization, they will not fare any better than those in the recent past. And decision-makers should not stop at proclaiming that they know what goes on and what must be done about it, because the will and motivation to do it may still be lacking. Our first objective must be to raise the level of human development in society, so as to enable people to see the changing world for themselves—and respond to what they see.

We must do everything to improve the sensitivity of the social organism to its changing environment. Reaction times must be shortened, and responses made more immediate and more to the point. This calls for providing for most people access to the necessary minimum of *education*; to free and unbiased channels of *communication*; and to relevant and reliable *information.*

Education, communication, and information are part of the reality of modern life, and those who buy and read books like the one now before the reader tend to take them for granted. However, the worldwide level and spread of education, communication, and information leave a great deal to be desired. Education bypasses the poor; communication is at most one way for the underprivileged; and information is largely irrelevant for many. It is not surprising that societies, like modern-day dinosaurs, fail to respond to their fast-changing environment.

THE PRIORITY REQUIREMENTS OF EDUCATION, COMMUNICATION, AND INFORMATION

Universal Education. Basic literacy—reading, writing, and numeral skills—is the rock bottom requirement if people are to evolve the ability to respond to the challenges of the world around them. Yet official estimates show over a billion illiterate people in the world, three quarters of them women. This figure, though staggering, is undoubtedly too low: States do not like to report high illiteracy rates, and experts do not have the means of counting the number of functional illiterates, the many individuals who were taught some rudimentary skills but do not know how to use them.

The great majority of today's illiterates are in the developing countries. The illiteracy rate reaches 65 percent of the total population in Africa, 36 percent in Asia, and 17 percent in Latin America and the Caribbean. In these areas the rapid growth in primary-school enrollment has ended; in some countries enrollment is actually declining. Statistics show that more than 100 million children of primary-school age are presently not enrolled in school. But there are no statistics showing how many are enrolled but not attending. Since lack of primary-school education is more pronounced among girls than among boys, the majority of adult illiterates are women.

Illiteracy interferes with all aspects of development: economic, social, human. Its impact on wealth creation is especially striking: In country after country, as illiteracy rates shoot up, per capita GNP plummets.

Overcoming the fateful literacy lag requires that disadvantaged segments of the population be given special attention: girls and women, children in nomadic and isolated communities, in deprived urban areas, and in refugee camps. As it is, more than one-fourth of contemporary humanity does not possess the minimum skills to absorb information beyond the spoken (if often radio-transmitted) word, and to communicate beyond face-to-face contact. Yet using farm and industrial

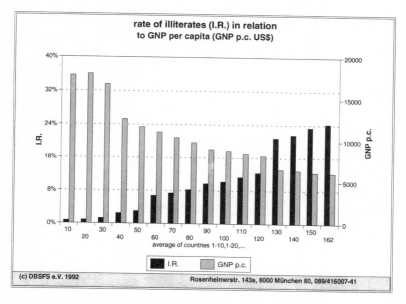

Illiteracy rate in relation to per capita GNP (average val-ues of groups of ten countries, in a total of 162 countries).

implements and undertaking community projects always call for some level of skill in reading, writing, and counting, the same as planning a family, raising children, and protecting the environment.

Basic education has become a universal problem, shared by almost all countries. Although worldwide some 98 percent of illiterate people live in the developing world, there are an estimated 20 million in the industrialized countries, besides a much larger number of functional illiterates. These numbers are inflated by immigration from the poor countries and are growing rapidly. In the Northern Hemisphere migrant illiterates live in especially demanding social and economic environments, and they constitute a pronounced liability to the social, economic, and political stability of their host country.

Action must be international, and taken on two fronts simultaneously: the provision of universal primary education for children joined with literacy and basic skill training for disadvantaged adults, and the creation of schools, curricula, and programs of continuing education to inform people of the essential elements of the local and global situation in which they find themselves.

Educational reform must encompass teacher training, curriculum development, the provision of teaching materials and technical aids, and, where needed, the building or renovating of schoolhouses and other infrastructures.

Unbiased Communication. Another priority requirement of human development concerns the nature and extent of the communications that develop in the contemporary world. As we noted in Chapter One, there has been unprecedented growth in the technologies of personal as well as mass communication in recent years. This is part of the informatization of the world. However, there has not been a significant reduction of the information gap between the developed and the developing countries, or between urban and rural environments. The fact that the number of communication channels has been increasing does not mean that the free flow of messages has been facilitated, or that whatever bias has been lodged in the messages has disappeared.

The messages that flow over today's globalized channels flow primarily one way. The three-fourths of the world population that inhabit the developing world find themselves at the receiving end of the flow. The messages they receive are hallmarked by the interests, values, and preoccupations of the privileged one-fourth, with distinctly limited relevance and utility for local life and experience. This is an irresponsible waste, for technologies of information and communication are much-needed channels of interpersonal communication and intercultural dialogue.

Globe-spanning communication systems can be used in a multitude of settings and in a diversity of cultural contexts. They can link men and women within one culture, and help them find their identity and role in life and society. They can link culture with culture, mitigating animosity, reducing the potential for conflict, and reinforcing mutual help and understanding. In addition to communicating the concepts and values of Westerners (which is what they are mostly made to do today), modern communication systems can convey the perceptions of Hindus, Buddhists, Moslems, Africans, and Confucians to one another, and to the other peoples and cultures of the world.

If the underprivileged three-fourths of the human population are to respond to the challenges of our rapidly changing world, the biased nature of modern communications needs to be rectified. This does not call for censorship, or for a "new international information and communication order," no matter how well intentioned such projects may be. Rather, it calls for real opportunities for the poor countries to develop their own communication infrastructures, public, private, or mixed. There must be financial, technical, and know-how support for the fledgling enterprises of the third-world communications sector; for training local journalists, communicators, and technicians; and for adapting the most suitable technologies to the limitations and capacities of the local environments.

In many cases it is rational to extend assistance to entire regions or subregions, for example, to East and West Africa, South Asia, Central America, and Oceania. Mechanisms for technical cooperation exist in these and other developing regions, but they are underfunded and largely inactive. They must be given more funds, clearer content, and definite objectives.

Relevant Information.   There is yet a third priority to be met if societies are to respond to the challenges of our time: the provision of relevant and factual information. If what people receive is largely irrelevant to their lives and circumstances, they will be misled or untouched by it. Basic education and two-way communication pay off only if the content of the received messages relates to the actual environments in which people live their lives and confront the challenges of existence.

There is a crucial difference between information that is irrelevant and in a practical sense all but useless; information that is relevant but biased; and information that is relevant and reasonably free of preconceptions. The difference is encapsulated in the oft-voiced request: "Just the facts, please." Here "just" indicates a request to do away with items that are irrelevant and useless, and the demand for "facts" means that the relevant and useful items are to be given without unnecessary—and possibly misleading—interpretation. If the three-fourths of humanity that are still primarily on the receiving end of the world's growing communication networks are to be given the opportunity to create and send messages that are of direct and vital interest to the entire human community, they must be given the facts, and only (or at least, mainly) the facts.

It is essential that the public and private organizations that define the nature and orientation of the information reaching a critical mass of the world's population be aware of the need to convey facts that are directly relevant to the problems and prospects of life in local settings. Like ensuring a free flow of information, this does not call for censorship and arbitrary screening: Items of general interest need not be neglected, or news concerning other peoples, societies, and cultures filtered out. The requirement is merely to complete the flow of information with items of direct relevance to the constraints, dangers, and opportunities that confront the recipients.

If a balanced mix is to be provided between entertainment and education, and foreign or general-interest items and items of direct local relevance, local and national information needs in the poor countries must be carefully analyzed and assessed. A properly balanced fare will foster effective self-help through a better understanding of local as well as world conditions. It will help people respond to the challenges they face locally, regionally, and nationally, without disregarding the context of the evolving world situation. This is a tall order, but it is the sine qua non of enabling today's societies to cope with their rapidly changing reality.

Evidently, human societies do not adapt as quickly and automatically to changing conditions as one might think. Although cultures and belief systems map and reinforce the experienced reality of a society—as the example of Sumerian, Egyptian, Hellenic, and Hebraic myths and religions show—cultures and belief systems do not emerge overnight. And, once they have emerged, they tend to be highly resistant to change. The religion of the Jews took many centuries to cohere into the doctrine of the Old Testament. The New Testament, though recounting the events of one short lifetime, took many centuries to become religious precept capable of infusing the thinking, feeling, and behavior of a significant number of people. The same held true for Islam, as well as for Hinduism, Taoism, Confucianism, Buddhism, and other oriental religions.

There are, in fact, three different rhythms of change in the human world, and there is a lag between all three. Biological evolution is slowest; cultural evolution is faster; and technology-triggered social evolution is the fastest. That biological evolution lags behind cultural and societal development is good: It permits successive generations to remain genetically stable while being culturally and technologically creative; it allows people to keep their bodies unchanged while changing their minds. But that cultures should lag behind technology-induced conditions could be dangerous. It prevents living generations from changing their minds fast enough to catch up with the social, economic, and environmental conditions their technologies have created.

The lag in today's culture with respect to technology-induced social change needs to be overcome. In this regard the importance of information can be hardly exaggerated. Information can trigger creativity, widen horizons, and enable people to adapt to the world in which they find themselves. Creating worldwide access to relevant information is a sound recipe for updating today's cultures and overcoming the dinosaur syndrome. It is the best way to enhance the responsiveness of peoples and societies, so that they can gain control of their destiny.

ACTION POINT: REASSESSING UNESCO

No state or government can tackle on its own the giant task of educating all the world's neglected people, and providing adequate information and communication facilities as well. This calls for broad-based international cooperation. Cooperation, in turn, calls for a central node in which the various strands of planning, decision, and implementation come together—not a world government, but a world-level coordinating body.

It so happens that in the aftermath of World War II the international community did create a world body in the areas of education, communication, and information, even if for most of the time since then—and especially in recent years—it has failed to make full use of it. That body is UNESCO, in whose name "E" stands for education, "C" for culture, and "S," though formally designating science, concerns the relevance and utility of scientific knowledge for contemporary people and societies.

The activities of UNESCO extend beyond the immediate domains of education, communication, and information, to the preservation of the cultural heritage of societies, the cultural identity of people, and the interaction between science, society, and the environment. But the brunt of UNESCO's activities focuses precisely on education, communication, and information.

Given the presence of an active coordination center mandated to promote activities in these fields, one may well ask how it is that the global picture remains as catastrophic as it is. Clearly, the effectiveness of UNESCO leaves much to be desired. Its inefficiency is often blamed on its being overly bureaucratized and politicized, and wasteful of its limited human and financial resources. This, however, is a simplification of the real state of affairs and requires reappraisal. A brief review of UNESCO's history and current programs gives a more balanced picture, better able to focus the needed action.

A Checkered History. UNESCO was founded in 1945 with the conviction that, while political and economic agreements are essential for lasting world peace, in and of themselves they are not a sufficient guarantee of it. Other foundations have to be laid as well, of a more intangible kind: respect for human rights and dignity and fundamental freedoms at all levels of life and society; recognition of the equal dignity and value of cultures in all their diversity; and individual and collective solidarity as a precondition of worldwide development.

Despite the noble aspirations of UNESCO's founders, the first forty years in the existence of the organization produced a checkered picture. In the late 1940s the world body got off to a flying start under the charismatic leadership of famed biologist Julian Huxley. In subsequent years, however, it could not avoid the ills that have beset other UN and world bodies: complex and slow decision-making procedures, cumbersome administrative setups, and a growing measure of politicization by its member states. While the organization chalked up notable successes in some areas, most visibly in the preservation of the tangible and intangible elements of the world's cultural heritage, it had less success in other domains, especially regarding education and communication in the developing countries. In 1988 a reassessment of the organization led to the decision to "go back to the sources," to the originally mandated responsibilities as the priority fields of activity.

The reasons for the reassessment were the various fears and criticisms expressed by member states, especially by the United States, the United Kingdom, and Singapore, the three states that in 1984 and 1985 decided to withdraw from UNESCO membership. Their criticism centered on the "New World Information and Communication Order": They feared that it would restrict freedom of the press internationally.

They also feared that universally accepted human rights would be downgraded as a result of concentrating on "people's rights." Major criticisms were directed at Amadou-Mahtar M'bow, the director-general at the time: He was said to concentrate too much power in his office, authorize budgetary excesses, and overconcentrate resources at the Paris headquarters.

In view of these and related problems, in 1984 UNESCO's executive board established a temporary committee to reform the organization and improve its functioning. The committee's thirteen recommendations dealt with the functioning of the governing organs; the decision-making process and the role of permanent delegations; program elaboration, implementation, and evolution; and management issues such as decentralization, personnel policy, public information, publications, operational activities, and budgetary matters. After 1987 the implementation of the committee's recommendations was taken over by the Special Committee, a permanent organ of UNESCO's executive board.

Current Ambitions. The Medium-Term Plan for 1990–1995, the third such plan in UNESCO's history, was prepared under the guidance of a new director-general who took office in November 1987. Federico Mayor, a Spanish biochemist with long experience in science and education policy, made clear that the plan is his absolute priority in efforts to refocus UNESCO's programs and introduce the necessary structural and management changes.

The plan sets clear limits on UNESCO's activities, concentrating only on those objectives that are directly consistent with its constitution. The organization was led away from debates on a New World Information and Communication Order in favor of implementing a strategy to "promote the free flow of ideas by word and image." The fourteen "major programmes" of the previous plan have been reduced to seven, and these center on UNESCO's mandated functions: education, the natural sciences, culture, communication, the social and human sciences; and related issues in the fields of development, human rights, and peace. Two major commissions have been established: the International Commission on Education and Learning for the Twenty-First Century, chaired by former European Community president Jacques Delors, and the World Commission on Culture and Development, headed by former UN secretary-general Javier Perez de Cuellar. The concentration of attention in a handful of priority areas permitted a significant reduction of expenditures, with the lion's share of the highly trimmed budget devoted to programs in basic education and literacy.

One of the most important and best financed of UNESCO's current programs is "Basic Education for All." It is funded and implemented jointly with the World Bank, UNDP, and UNICEF, with the objective of promoting literacy and basic learning for adults, and universal primary education for children. The stated intent is to eradicate illiteracy by the year 2000. The world conference on this topic, held in March 1990 in Jomtien, Thailand, was a milestone in UN interagency cooperation. The final statement called for a new strategy to move education into a priority position in national development planning, and backed what it called the "expanded vision" with more than $2 billion in funds, including a $1.5 billion contribution by the World Bank.

Further UNESCO programs worthy of note include: "Education for the 21st Century," with particular emphasis on environmental education, education to control drug abuse and the spread of AIDS, science education, as well as certain facets of higher education. Another program integrates health care and educational services for population segments at highest risk: mothers, young children, and infants. In the field of communication, activity is keyed to the concept of "communication for development," in the conviction that effective assistance for building communication capabilities in developing countries must embrace the entire process from project planning through technology choice and personnel training, all the way to the production and preservation of programs and materials. The goal is to create new channels and dialogue where significant gaps appear, so that developing countries can communicate with one another as well as with the industrialized world. In addition to strengthening communication capacities in developing countries, the strategy encourages the free flow of information throughout the world at national as well as international levels, and promotes a wider and better balanced dissemination of information without restricting the freedom of expression.

Still other UNESCO programs and activities concern the safeguarding of the integrity of the world's cultures. The 1988–1997 "World Decade for Cultural Development," in addition to attempting to affirm and enrich cultural identities, aims at acknowledging the cultural dimension of development; assuring a broader participation of people in cultural life; and promoting international cooperation in the field of culture.

What Next? As this overview indicates, UNESCO is active in practically all the domains where priority action is called for in the interest of overcoming the dinosaur syndrome. The fact that many societies remain sluggish nevertheless, confirms that UNESCO, the world organization mandated to promote and coordinate action in the pertinent fields, is not operating at the required level of effectiveness and efficiency. This, however, does not mean that UNESCO has to be abandoned; it could mean that it has to be revitalized.

UNESCO is still plagued by a number of problems and constraints. The most important among them are:

- An uncertain consensus among member states. An intergovernmental organization is dependent on agreement among its member states regarding the goals it should pursue and the methods it should adopt to pursue them. While there has been real progress in this regard since the mid-eighties, when UNESCO was all but torn asunder by dissent, the process remains delicate and uncertain, with occasional blockages that only consummate skill on the part of the director-general can resolve.

- A small and highly earmarked budget. The budget problems that plague most international organizations are felt especially keenly at UNESCO. The current regular budget of just over $47 million a year is not higher than that of a medium-sized U.S. university, and how it is spent is overseen by cost-conscious member states down to the last penny.
- A highly diverse staff. People from more than 130 countries work for UNESCO at its Paris headquarters and various field offices. While this contributes an international and intercultural dimension to the staff, it poses many problems of interpersonal and intersectoral cooperation and adds a great deal of complexity to the tasks of management and administration.

What next indeed? The issues of education, communication, and information, the same as intercultural understanding and pertinent scientific knowledge, are too important to be postponed or put on the back burner. Progress in the fields of education, communication, and information is essential if solutions to global problems are to be effectively tackled. This calls for some measure of world-level coordination in program design and implementation. There is a world body mandated to work in this very area, with an efficient Director-General re-elected in 1993. But this body still faces resource, procedural, and credibility problems. This can and must be rectified.

Strengthening UNESCO and making it more effective and efficient calls, as the U.S. and the U.K. have now recognized, for full participation and support by the international community. This, in turn, requires a wider awareness of the issues in the public, with purposively orchestrated campaigns by leaders in education, communication, and public-spirited business. The results would have a surprising potential for pay-off: There is hardly another area of international action that is as cost-effective as education, information, and communication.

9

An Agenda for World Order

In the 1970s third-world governments, nongovernmental organizations, and UN debates were full of doctrinaire and mostly unrealistic projects for a new international economic as well as information and communication order. Today, creating a new order on the global scale must not be a doctrinaire and need not be an unrealistic proposition. Rising concerns with the environment, the activities of global corporations, the stability of the world financial system, and the promotion of worldwide economic development, joined with enduring concerns for international peace and security, bring fresh motivation to global issues and their governance. The winding down of the cold war is liberating energies, and could also liberate funds, to put the required mechanisms in place. The time is ripe for advancing realistic agendas for a flexible and just world-level order.

THREE SCENARIOS

The critical relevance of world-order concepts is highlighted by the realization that the alternative to some functional form of global order is either a one-sided dictatorship of the rich and powerful, or unbridled and potentially disastrous competition between the rich and the powerful and the poor and the powerless. The following global scenarios illustrate the prospects.

Scenario 1: The first scenario is optimistic but naive: It foresees a smooth continuation of present trends far into the twenty-first century. This would greatly exacerbate the current gap between the rich and the poor, creating widening gaps between entire continents. Already by the year 2010, the gap would be wide enough to surpass all expectations of assured peace and stability.

In regard to its specifics, the first scenario may go something like this. In its initial, smoothly evolving phase, a number of developing-country economies, first and foremost China, enter the world economy as major players. They export cheap manufactured goods, use increasing energies and raw materials, and produce large increments of waste and pollution. Competition intensifies for increasingly scarce resources, even for habitable space and agricultural lands. As population follows its likely growth-curve, the environment suffers. Besides pollution, waste disposal becomes a worldwide problem: No nation is willing anymore to be a dumping ground for others.

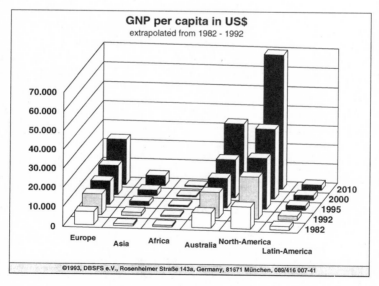

GNP per capita by continent, extrapolated on the basis of evolution from 1982 to 1991 (in U.S. dollars).

Toxic wastes end up wherever national supervision is lax or lacking—for the most part in the "global commons": the oceans and the polar regions.

Before long, the smooth developmental curve of the scenario inflects. The global mercantilism of the 1990s transforms into open economic warfare. The major companies cope for a while with innovative strategies: They restructure themselves, reposition their market presence, merge with more powerful players and even with competitors, and diversify their product line. Many go bankrupt, but cleverer or more opportunistic players take their place. The surviving corporations employ increasingly ruthless tactics to cope with opportunistic and corrupt rivals. High unemployment, inflation, and unpredictable currency fluctuations make for an every-company-for-itself, survive-or-perish corporate philosophy.

In the public domain, governments have less flexibility. Only the richest are able to satisfy the demands placed on them. Employment opportunities and welfare programs for the poor are among the first to suffer; shantytowns, favelas, and street people multiply in and around dozens of big cities. Economic volatility and impotence in regard to controlling it dominate policy. Under intensifying pressure, governmental action becomes frenzied and ad hoc. The state intervenes in the market with stopgap regulations; it concludes alliances that neither the government nor the contracting partners are prepared to maintain if and when they no longer serve their immediate interests. On the streets of third-world megalopolises ever more force needs to be employed to quell riots and maintain order; in country after country, more public money is spent to build up police and security forces and construct prisons and detention camps.

Every attempt to overcome a crisis brings further problems in its wake. Many of the 200-odd states of the twenty-first century become ungovernable. In the business world competition moves beyond self-restraint and escapes public regulation. In the end, the global system becomes critically unstable. Any small spark—the shutdown of a plant, an unfair tax, a canceled benefit—can ignite a flame. Local fires flare up in region after region, and the tragedy of Bosnia-Herzegovina is played out, continent after continent. Before long, the forces of unrest exceed the ability of national, regional, and global peacekeeping forces to reestablish and maintain peace and order.

As unrest spreads and escalates, the results are unforeseeable. National arsenals, no longer subject to international verification, stockpile nuclear, chemical, biological, and conventional weapons. Their use remains the last resort of the world's otherwise impotent governments.

Scenario 2: This future is likewise pessimistic, and only a shade less realistic than scenario 1. It takes its cue from the latter. In anticipation of spreading public unrest and economic breakdown, the major economic and military powers of the world join forces to create a defensive global alliance. The world of the twenty-first century transforms into an arena where a handful of economic-political power blocs are the dominant gladiators. One such bloc is the Europe of the enlarged Community: It extends from the Atlantic to the Urals. Another brings together the United States with Canada and Mexico: This bloc evolves out of NAFTA, the North American Free Trade Agreement. A third bloc forms if and when Japan realizes that it is not accepted on equal terms into the alliance of North America—it then turns to its Asia-Pacific partners to conclude a wide range of economic cooperation treaties, backed up by mutual security alliances.

Today the three regions—the European, the North American, and the Asia-Pacific—produce 73 percent of world GNP. Within a decade they dominate the world economy. They control most of the world's resources and almost all of its industry. Trade among them accounts for the overwhelming portion of global trade. Other countries are unable to compete, although China and the South American economic blocs—based on Mercosur and the Andean Pact—secure specific niches in global markets. But most parts of Africa and South

Asia sink into poverty: Trade with them becomes unprofitable and investment insecure.

The world's population divides into highly disparate economic zones. As the rich—in absolute numbers a shrinking minority—become still richer while the poor continue to get children, the former get together to take control of the situation before it is too late. The three dominant blocs establish a global currency, which they jointly control. They set rules for manufacture and trade, and for permissible environmental impact. The intent of the ruling powers is humanistic, though they cannot afford to be altruistic: In an overpopulated, resource-hungry, and inequitably endowed world, naive benevolence is unforgiving. Though global measures are accompanied by ample declarations that they will bring benefit to everyone, the more than four-fifths of the world's peoples who are outside the dominant power blocs experience a growing sense of oppression and injustice.

As contact between the world's peoples and economies intensifies, disparities between the living standards of the concert of European, North American, and Asia-Pacific powers and the rest of the world become more evident, and hence offensive. It is only a matter of time before public perceptions cross the fateful threshold that divides tolerance from revolt. The frustrated and marginalized majority rises up against the privileged minority. Attempts to turn Europe, North America, and the Asia-Pacific into protected fortresses are condemned to fail; vast borders cannot be protected from the influx of migrants any more than air and water can be protected from the inflow of pollutants. The central-powers-dominated global security systems breaks down, and with it the global economic system. From here on, scenario 2 becomes a replay of the final phases of scenario 1.

We can now turn to *scenario 3*. It is more desirable than the other two, and, if we act wisely, also more faithful to what will actually happen. This scenario foresees a determined movement toward a global commonwealth, based on international and intercultural consensus, with collective efforts to safeguard the balances essential for the functioning of the world's social and economic system, combined with phased reductions in the major socioeconomic gaps and inequities.

Scenario 3 requires suitable world-level coordination and decision-making mechanisms. They are needed to make sure that the third scenario does not telescope into the second, and then collapse into the first.

Functional world-order mechanisms do not grow overnight, and they cannot be trusted to grow merely by a fortunate coincidence of circumstances. Launching and operating them calls for insight into the evolutionary trend and conscious effort to go with it, making use of the will and motivation that is generated by insight into necessity.

A functional world order can be built by selectively furthering and purposefully guiding the processes that mark the unfolding of the evolutionary trend. This involves:

- the intensification of convergence or integration in various world regions;
- the identification and limitation of the domains where world-level decisions are to be taken; and
- the creation of adequate mechanisms for world-level decision-making and implementation.

FURTHERING CONVERGENCE

National governments are caught in the jaws of a dilemma: whether to hold on to all possible dimensions of their national sovereignty, or to selectively transfer some sovereign rights to international and intergovernmental organizations.

The former alternative currently proves to have more appeal. The idea that the nation-state is sovereign has not lost much of its power over the centuries. In most parts of the world it is still dominant.

The classical concept of the nation-state appeared in its still operative juridical form in the year 1648, in the Peace of Westphalia. The concept ascribed full sovereignty to the people of a nation-state, a sovereignty that today is exercised by representative governments. The sovereignty of democratic states extends to all facets of their territory and its resources. The government of a sovereign state is alone responsible for its actions within its sphere of sovereignty; it does not recognize any international authority. Though long overtaken by globalizing processes in the economy, the sovereign nation-state is still the de jure apex of social, political, and even economic organization on Earth. Blind adherence to it could become a major roadblock to evolutionary convergence in the human community.

We should note, however, that the evolutionary trend does not drive solely toward more embracing economic, social, and political systems; it also catalyzes growing differentiation among the grass-roots subsystems. Today's societies evolve, as societies always did, through a twofold process made up on the one hand of integration, and on the other of articulation.

There is no contradiction here between the dissolution of the Soviet Union and Yugoslavia on the one hand, and the integration of European states within a Europe-wide community on the other. Convergence means that existing societies tend to integrate among themselves, establishing closer, more symbiotic ties with one another. This also involves articulation, the process whereby the regional and ethnic components of societies become more and more distinct and autonomous.

Integration is not uniformization, the domination of one element and the subordination of others. It is the coordination of all elements in a shared and mutually beneficial order. Thus integration does not flatten cultural diversity, it only orchestrates it.

Throughout history, the integration and articulation elements of evolutionary convergence were occasionally out of kilter. Today, the world is in need of shifting its evolutionary dynamics to favor integration. Interdependence has grown too fast for contemporary societies in Europe, as well as in Africa, Asia, and Latin America. They were pushed into one another's arms without being ready for the close embrace. In consequence, the international system lapsed into disorder, its level of integration insufficient to coordinate its economic, political, and ethnic differentiation.

The facts speak to this point. There are more than 190 nation-states in our increasingly interdependent human community, ranging from economic and technological giants such as the United States, Japan, and Germany, and from demographic giants such as the People's Republic of China, India, and Brazil, to such poor and small countries as Guinea, Mauritania, Benin, and scores of others on the UN's list of least developed states. There are several hundred global-reach business corporations that hold unprecedented wealth and wield unprecedented power; and there are a handful of nuclear powers that store enough explosives in their arsenals to wipe out not only their perceived adversaries, but all of humanity. This system has grown ungovernable: It must now tilt the seesaw toward integration.

Tilting toward integration is important for all states, in all parts of the world. To integrate themselves without loss of identity is a vital challenge for the European states, members of the European Community. It is an entirely paramount requirement for third-world countries, for example, the members of the Andean Pact and the Association of South-East Asian States. It is likewise important for East European states such as Russia, the Ukraine, Latvia, and Croatia, since they need dependable economic and political ties with one another, in addition to a new identity and a higher level of autonomy.

Furthering the processes of convergence through regional integration is an important step on the long and complex road leading toward a realistic and noncoercive world order.

Regional bodies can arbitrate regional conflict and equilibrate regional processes; they can create a higher level of stability and self-reliance in their area than uncoordinated nation-states. Regional balance and stability, in turn, are essential for averting the massive waves of migrants that would otherwise flood the more developed parts of a region, as well as the more developed parts of neighboring regions. Unless Europe manages to integrate the former socialist states within a reasonably developed and balanced economic community, the more privileged members of that community will expose themselves to giant waves of immigration from the East. And, unless also the North African states manage to build a reasonably successful and balanced economic community among themselves, Europe will be flooded by waves of immigrants from the South.

A similar problem in the Western Hemisphere can be averted by promoting the regional development of the Latin American countries, and in Asia by allowing the East and South Asian nations to pursue their own developmental path.

The desirable world order of *Scenario 3* can be achieved in reality by furthering international convergence, both on the regional level in the form of economic communities, and on the global level, through the interregional integration of the existing regional communities. If all countries of the world community participate in regional development, Scenario 3 will not degenerate into the power-hierarchy of Scenario 2, with the consequent danger of collapsing into the chaos of Scenario 1.

We should be clear that a lasting and equitable world order is not likely to be built on voluntary accords between 190 highly unequal, and in large part also highly unstable, nation-states. It is also not likely to endure as a hierarchy where a few rich power-blocs dominate many weaker and poorer nation-states or groups of states. A lasting world order requires more balanced foundations. These can be built by furthering the evolutionary process of convergence both regionally and interregionally.

THE DOMAINS OF DECISION-MAKING

A fundamental precondition of creating a functional world order is being able to decide just where this order is to hold sway, and where not. The domains where global-level decision-making is called for must be defined and carefully limited. This can be done in reference to the so-called subsidiarity principle, affirmed among others by the InterAction Council at its Lisbon meeting in April 1990. The urgently needed new world order, said the former heads of state and government who make up the membership of the council, "must be characterized by the exercise of delegated sovereignty based on the principle that decisions should be taken at the lowest possible level at which they can be effective."

There are many areas where the lowest possible level of decision-making is the local, and on these areas grass-roots decisions are indicated. Other areas call for national decision-making, and still others for regional mechanisms. But there are also areas where the lowest possible level at which decisions could be effective is the global. These areas, as noted in Chapter One, include humanitarian relief as well as international peace and security, the management of the global environment, and the regulation of the world financial system.

The need for global-level decision-making is especially urgent in the area of security. While the climate for international peacekeeping has improved, existing mechanisms remain inadequate for the tasks of maintaining world peace. In a world of growing ecological stresses, financial instabilities, significantly reduced political tensions, and demonstrated military impotence, some national governments continue to dream of military superiority. Together they spend close to $1,000 billion annually on armaments and military establishments, and only a fraction of that sum on collective peacekeeping, a safe environment, and a sound financial system.

Prolonging this situation could be dangerous: It risks increasing social and economic instability, perceived injustice, and ultimately violence. There is an urgent need for binding international accords leading to firm commitments among participating governments to a collective security and peace-keeping system. Such a system would allow, and more than that, it would *require* its members to contain their own military arsenals.

At the present time collective peacekeeping by the UN is uncertain and underfunded. The UN Charter provides for the creation of an enforcement mechanism to carry out collective measures approved by the Security Council, but under such authority only a handful of enforcement operations and less than two dozen nonenforcement or "peacekeeping" operations were carried out in the UN's fifty-year history. Though they were for the most part successful, they were usually perilously fragile: The system had neither an adequate financial basis to execute them, nor the staff to manage the operations.

Now that the U.S.S.R. is no longer there to block Security Council decisions, there is an urgent need to improve UN capability in the security domain. There is a need to create a state-of-the-art monitoring and early-warning capability to advise the Security Council of incipient dangers. With an international team of supervisors at the helm, the monitoring facility could enable the council to head off crises before they erupt into violence.

For the Security Council to have the power to make the required decisions, and also to be able to enforce them, it would have to have an adequately funded and equipped military force at its command. This corps of "soldiers without enemies" would have to be thoroughly trained, securely funded, and continually ready for action.

In the ecologic area, adequate instruments are just as needed as in the security domain. The urgency of global environmental actions is generally recognized, but the funds required to finance them are not forthcoming. The Rio "Earth Summit," while it has raised consciousness of the issues, did not raise significant money to cope with them. And the political will to create, and if necessary enforce, meaningful environmental action is still lacking. Yet, as many experts and some governments already recognize, if current disastrous trends are to be turned around, there must be a global-level body mandated to carry out a number of key functions. These functions include:

- monitoring and assessing environmental impacts;
- providing early warning in the event of impending crises;
- delivering emergency aid and relief;
- arbitrating the resolution of actual or potential conflicts; and
- coordinating and supervising the implementation of the agreed measures.

To assure a proper execution of the above functions, another small but expert army would be needed, this time not of blue but of *green* berets. And this army of "soldiers of nature" would have to be equally well funded and well equipped, and ready for action throughout the lands and oceans of the biosphere.

Last but not least, consideration must be given to an effective instrument to stabilize and balance global financial flows. The world financial system needs to be protected from such crises as are periodically due to ad hoc deregulation, new financial instruments, the introduction of new markets (such as the futures market), and the instant, worldwide, computer-based linkage of markets, instruments, and currencies.

The goals that a world financial authority would have to pursue include facilitation of the settlement of international trade disputes; creation of access for countries with export-led economies to markets with real purchasing power; and limitation of the extreme concentration of transnational direct investment to Europe, North America, and Japan. The world body would have to set universal rules for services and cross-border investments and to phase in the reduction of tariff and nontariff barriers to trade. It would have to coordinate the market interventions of central banks in order to avoid confusion and create greater transparency. And it would need to create a set of standards based on principles of neutrality, regulatory independence, harmonization, inclusiveness, transparency, and mutual recognition.

In addition to such technical (but strongly public-interest) objectives, global coordination in the financial sphere could be made to bring benefits of a more tangible kind. It could prove effective in counteracting the current population explosion. Although ultimately national population growth rates would reduce spontaneously, as higher levels of socioeconomic development drop the real and perceived need for large families, growth rates could be reduced much quicker by tying certain elements of international capital flows to demographic measures to be undertaken by the recipient-country governments. For example, access to direct investment capital could be facilitated in exchange for more effective social insurance schemes, public information campaigns, and the distribution of contraceptive devices among high-fertility populations.

The prospect of a string of international organizations regulating more and more aspects of human activity fills many people with misgivings. Citizens fear the specter of distant and unfeeling bureaucracies issuing edicts and influencing their lives, and governments fear having to yield further elements of the sovereignty they consider their inalienable right. However, fears of world bodies and reluctance to create them would not be justified if the institutional mechanisms confine themselves to the handful of domains where measures are irremediably ineffective unless decided and executed on the global level. A global peacekeeping system, an ecologic authority, and a financial regulatory body would serve every nation's interest. They would not impair the autonomy of national and local decision-making in other policy domains.

World-order mechanisms must be created if the breakdowns of scenarios 1 and 2 are to be avoided. Properly conceived and administered, they could be cost-effective, and the burden of maintaining them could be distributed throughout the international community, with due regard for need, benefit, as well as ability to pay.

ACTION POINT: REFORMING THE UN

The currently needed world-order bodies could be set up within the UN system or outside of it. There are pros and cons associated with either option. *Outside* the UN system the new bodies would enjoy complete independence and autonomy. Their actions could, however, suffer from the tunnel vision that comes with highly focused sectoral approaches. *Within* the UN the new bodies would be subject to the political constraints that exist within that system, but they would also be exposed to the need to harmonize their policies with those of the other agencies. Given the urgency of the issues, and the cumbersome negotiations required to build international institutions from scratch, the UN option appears considerably wiser. It calls, however, for a thorough reform of the UN system.

First of all, if the UN were to be the seat of a string of new world bodies, the restriction of its membership to national states would have to be lifted. Regional integration organizations such as the EC, ASEAN, etc., would have to represent their members and articulate their intentions. This would considerably simplify debate, negotiation, and voting procedures. Major business companies would also have to be represented, with full negotiating and voting privileges. Such representation could be either by worldwide industry branch or by regional industry association. And UN membership would have to be extended to nongovernmental organizations as well, representing relevant professional bodies, universities, research institutes, churches, and other public-interest nongovernmental institutions.

Second, the secretariat would have to reconstitute itself in a creative and efficient fashion. It would have to evolve an

integrated operating capability, overcoming the current fragmentation of the authority of the secretary-general among diverse departments, divisions, and specialized agencies. Some
UN departments and agencies compete rather than cooperate
with one another, while others, like the members of the World
Bank Group, are only token parts of the system. The heads of
the World Bank and the IMF appear in cabinet meetings and at
the Economic and Social Council, but their appearances are
mainly symbolic: These powerful bodies are led by their own
governing bodies (which are dominated by the wealthy nations) and do not subject themselves to substantive coordination by the system either at the intergovernmental or at the
secretariat level. Other UN organs tend to take unilateral action as well, in particular UNCTAD, a specialized agency that
in turn is dominated by the poor countries.

Since the end of the 1960s, the UN system has been the subject of numerous studies and discussions, by both individual
scholars and formally mandated commissions. The transformation of the system from a loosely knit set of semi-
independent and frequently competing subunits to an organic
whole serving the world community has been an integral element of the reports of these groups. But the majority of the
recommendations, including those framed by the Jackson and
the Pierson Reports, focused on the efficiency of the organization and on procedural and organizational issues, assuming
that the basic tasks have been adequately defined in the charter. Yet, as Federico Mayor, the director-general of UNESCO,
pointed out at a cabinet meeting in April 1991, it is no longer
enough to confine efforts to try to make the system more effective; it is also necessary to make it more relevant. There is an
urgent need to establish the priority areas of action, and
within them to distinguish at least three categories of tasks:
those that the system can carry out by itself; those that call for
interventions requiring extra financing; and those that call
only for guidance or coordination.

The question of relevance would be answered by creating

within the UN authoritative bodies with specific mandates in the fields of security, environment, and finance. The question of funding would also have to be resolved. Part of the financing would be assured by earmarking funds saved from national budgets that became superfluous as the new bodies came online. These funds are not likely to be sufficient, however, to enable the new bodies to respond to their broader mandates in going beyond consultation and advisory functions to full-scale negotiations, implementation, and the redressment of problems arising from implementation.

To fund enforcement and peacekeeping operations, member states would have to earmark part of their defense budgets for the purpose. Currently UN budget assessments are calculated on each member's share of the gross world product. (The share of the United States is the highest: 25 percent.) A sound financial basis would require that the system be revised to have member states pay a quota fixed in proportion to their current *military* expenditures. This system of financing would not only create funds that are proportional to the need for collective peacekeeping, which is to maintain a joint capability that is superior to the security threat posed by armed aggression by individual states. It would also encourage member states to make progressive cuts in their national military budgets (since the lower their budget, the more they would save on their contribution). If, for example, the United States provided an annual $25 billion from its estimated nearly $300 billion military expenditures, and if the other major military powers also paid up their share, the Security Council would have an active $100 billion mechanism at its command. This would be sufficient to respond to the international community's diverse monitoring, early-warning, peacekeeping, and enforcement requirements. And it would relieve the United States of the far more costly preparedness that goes with being policeman to the world.

Like the peacekeeping system, global ecologic operations would cost money; but ways of raising the necessary funds exist there as well. As environmentalists often emphasize, some level of financing could be raised by taxing the use of the global commons. Taxing the use of regions outside sovereign national territories would have multiple benefits. It would discourage overexploitation by making it more expensive, and the revenues thus collected could underwrite the cost of a string of cleanup and safeguard operations.

The oceans, the arctic regions, the atmosphere, and outer space are properly considered "the collective heritage of humankind." They need not any longer be treated as a free resource, to be exploited by whoever has the power and the technology to do so. Exploitation should be duly paid for, with the benefits administered by an organization that represents the collective interests of the human community.

Financial operations would not require high-level financing: They would mostly consist of expert monitoring and decision-making. Once governments have committed themselves to abide by the decisions, the budget for the monitoring and decision-making mechanism could be assembled from subscriptions by member states, with individual quotas established in light of national wealth and development. Contributions could be scaled proportionately. Poor and underdeveloped countries would have insignificantly low subscription quotas, and while the rich countries would pay more, the benefits of a reliable financial system would outweigh the burden of higher payments.

For the UN to become an operational center of decision and action in key world-order domains, its crucial operations would have to be adequately and dependably financed, and the system as a whole would have to become universal in representation and membership. It would also have to be better coordinated than today, less politicized, and more authoritative in decision-making and in the field.

Achieving these goals presupposes a great deal of energy and creativity on the part of the secretary-general; commitment and solidarity by the executive officers of the various bodies, divisions, and agencies; and flexibility and political will on the part of a wider and more representative national, regional, and nongovernmental membership.

Understanding, and eventually support, would not be lacking by the major member states. In the United States, for example, a recent poll, reported in May 1993 by the Americans Talk Issues Foundation, revealed that 80 percent of registered voters are in favor of the UN taking responsibility for international security; 74 percent are for the organization being given responsibility for world environmental problems; and 62 percent would support calling a world conference to overhaul the UN's original, and now increasingly obsolete, 1945 charter.

Though a large order, UN reform is no longer utopian. The ending of the superpower confrontation offers the world community a unique opportunity to create the mechanisms for a sustainable and fair world order. These center above all on human development, international security, a healthy environment, and realistic financing for socioeconomic development.

IV

THE OUTLOOK

10

Signs of Hope

Will we choose evolution or extinction as our destiny? The answer is not yet in, but there are signs of hope. New modes of thinking and valuing appear in society; they augur new and more adapted ways of behaving.

Of course, patterns of thought and action have always changed in history, from society to society and generation to generation. But in former times change was slow and mainly local. Today, impelled by technological innovation and fed by global flows of information and communication, value and behavior change is accelerating and spreading to every part of the world.

The current wave of change started in the 1960s at the periphery, with the women's movement and the new age and early green movements. It rose toward the center of the establishment in the 1970s and eighties with the maturing of the environmental and the social welfare movements. By the 1990s the great majority of industrialized societies have been caught up in it. It is affecting the thinking and behavior of citizens as well as of consumers; governments and businesses have begun to pay attention to it.

Value Change in Society. The fact that value change should be spreading and accelerating is not surprising: Our dominant values and worldviews were shaped by the experience of national industrial societies, and as that kind of social and economic system has been disappearing, the concepts suggested by our daily experience are exposed to question. Those we are especially reluctant to give up are in danger of becoming obsolete.

In industrialized countries, more and more people are rethinking such basic concepts as those concerning the nature of self-interest, efficiency, the distribution of wealth, the value of specialists, and the role of values and beliefs. They question, for example:

- that those who survive are necessarily the ones who are the strongest. Could it be that the survivors are those who are the most symbiotic with their fellow humans and with nature?

- that true efficiency is simply maximum productivity. Would efficiency lie more in the creation of humanly necessary and socially useful goods and services?

- that the trickle-down theory is true, so that when the rich get richer, the poor are better off as well. Is it not more effective to help the poor and underprivileged by creating better conditions for them and better opportunities for finding meaningful work?

- that our problems can be best solved by experts who specialize in the issues before them. Is it not true that specialists know more and more about less and less, with the result that they are exposed to unexpected consequences and perhaps to vexing side effects as processes in one sphere cross-impact with those in others in our interdependent world?

- that ideas, values, and beliefs are the luxuries of those who can afford them, good for impressing spouses and associates, but for little else. Could it be that what we value and how we view the world have a vital role by paving the way for the social and cultural innovations that are the preconditions of progress in times of uncertainty and change?

The way people view nature, themselves, other people, and social processes is changing rapidly. The map of the world we carry in our heads is no longer what it was ten years ago. At that time not many would have questioned beliefs such as the above, and even fewer would have thought of the alternatives we now envisage.

Green Trend in Politics. Until about 1988, the governments of the industrialized countries underplayed environmental issues, fearing negative impacts on economic growth and global competitiveness. The East European regimes rejected ecologic measures outright: There can be no environmental degradation under Socialism. Third-world governments, in turn, proclaimed that environmental problems are due to the industrialized nations, and they must take the responsibility for coping with them.

Then, in 1988 the public media seized on the environment as a topic of major interest. Within a single twelve-month period the National Geographic Society published *Earth '88;* *Time* magazine devoted its 1989 New Year's edition to "Earth, Planet of the Year"; *The Economist* came out with a special survey on "Costing the Earth"; *Scientific American* dedicated an issue to "Managing Planet Earth"; and *The New Yorker* published a thirty-five-page article titled "The End of Nature." People responded. In the United States, the proportion of those who thought that environmental improvements must be made "regardless of cost" rose by a quarter in a matter of months. In Britain, where the September 1988 publication of *The Green Consumer Guide* sparked intense debate, the proportion of people who said that they bought a product because it was "friendly to the environment" doubled within a year. People learned to ask for aerosols that did not contain CFCs, detergents that were free of phosphates, and beef that had not been grazed on cleared rain forest.

As public opinion came around, politicians were quick to note the changed mood. Almost half of Margaret Thatcher's September 1988 speech to the Royal Society was devoted to the issue of environmental imbalances and the need to accept the concept of sustainable economic development. In his

December 1988 speech to the UN, Mikhail Gorbachev spoke of the ecologic catastrophe that would follow on traditional types of industrialization; Queen Beatrix of the Netherlands dedicated her entire Christmas speech to the nation to environmental threats confronting life on earth. In the summer of 1989, green parties won two dozen seats in the European Parliament. In the United States, George Bush appointed a pro-

OUR CHANGING BELIEFS

The Old	The New
The Human/Nature Relation	
Human beings are masters of nature, controlling natural processes, plants, and animals for their own higher purposes.	Humans are an organic part within the self-maintaining and self-evolving orders of the biosphere and must not step beyond their natural limits.
The Male-Female Relation	
Society is male dominated and therefore hierarchical, using high concentrations of power and wealth as the way to promote male-designated interests and maintain male-concentrated affluence.	Sharing and complementarity between women and men have priority over top-down command structures in all areas of the private as well as the professional sphere.
Competition vs. Cooperation	
The economy is an arena for struggle and survival; the coincidence of individual and public good can be entrusted to Adam Smith's "invisible hand."	Cooperation is a higher value than competition; the profit and power-hunger of the modern work ethos must be tempered with the valuation of individual differences.

fessional environmentalist (William Reilly, former president of the World Wildlife Fund) to his cabinet as Administrator of EPA, the Environmental Protection Agency. Since 1993, in the Clinton administration, the election of environmental advocate Al Gore to the vice presidency made environmental policy more informed and influential.

Though in most parts of the world ecopolitics remains

(continued from page 182)

The Old	**The New**
Fragmentation vs. Wholeness	
Objects are separate from their environments; people are separate from one another and replaceable in their social and economic functions.	There are constant and close connections between people, and between people and nature, calling for due emphasis on community and solidarity in both the human and the natural world.
Accumulating vs. Sustaining	
The accumulation of material goods is the pinnacle of achievement and success, regardless of its costs in energy, raw materials, and human and natural resources.	Sustainability is a central value, and calls for flexibility and mutual accommodation among people as well as between people and their natural environment.

confused and short-term oriented, and secretaries and ministers of the environment have less power than other cabinet members, the ecology is one of the few areas where public-sector governance is on the way to becoming globalized. Given the higher visibility and the increasing cost of environmental

THE SHIFT IN CORPORATE CULTURE

The Old	**The New**

Hierarchic vs. Distributed Decision-Making

The enterprise must function as a disciplined hierarchy in which top management decides all parameters of planning and operation.	Information and decision-making are to be decentralized through networklike structures in which the people closest to a given job have the responsibility of deciding how best it is to be performed.

Control vs. Self-regulation

Rigorous external controls must be applied to all phases of work, using supervisors, specialists, and if possible automated control procedures.	Semiautonomous task forces and worker teams can be entrusted with self-control and self-discipline, within networked and largely self-governing subdivisions.

Machine vs. Human

The human being is an unreliable extension of unerring and reliable machines; he/she should be replaced with automation whenever and wherever possible.	The human being is a crucial factor in all phases of corporate operation, irreplaceable by even the best computers and computer-governed systems.

problems, the weight of green policies is likely to increase, on national, regional, as well as global levels.

Shifts in Corporate Culture. The world of business is exhibiting signs of a major shift in what has become known as "cor-

---

(continued from page 184)

The Old	**The New**
Routine Tasks vs. Responsible Jobs	
All phases of human labor are best broken down into simple and narrow skills, mechanizing the work process and making it maximally controllable and dependable.	Corporate personnel are to be assigned broad tasks and responsibilities, matching their dispositions and their manual and intellectual capacities.
Complementary Sex Roles	
Women are best for unskilled or semiskilled jobs, in performing routine tasks in the assembly line, in secretarial positions, and in cleaning up.	Women are to be brought into all levels of job performance and responsibility, drawing on the essential complementarity of female and male personalities, skills, and concerns.
The Business of Business	
The business of business is business; all else is window-dressing, needed for good consumer and public relations.	The business of business is the good of its employees, its suppliers, and customers; in the last count, the good of society as a whole.

porate culture." The changes mirror value change in society, but focus on issues that are of direct relevance to modern enterprises within their complex economic, political, social, and ecologic environments.

Benchmarks of the corporate culture shift are evident in all spheres of company activity and organization. For example:

Organizational modality has gone from hierarchy to a networklike structure.

Leadership style has changed from autocratic to distributed within the organization.

The corporate structure went from closure in regard to alteration, to growing innovation-friendliness.

The definition of objectives has moved from top management to a broad circle of collaborators.

The competitive edge is no longer uniquely cost saving and productivity increase, but R&D, innovation, and time saving.

The focus of management has shifted from exclusive attention to profit and market share to quality and customer satisfaction.

The key resource has shifted in turn from capital availability: It is now people and information.

Work force expectation has been changing from sole concern with financial security to meaningful employment and personal growth.

The corporate culture-shift has had the greatest impact in the area of the environment. Managers who had looked on environmentalists as long-haired radicals discovered that their profits depended heavily on whether their products are "environmentally friendly"—nontoxic, biodegradable, recycled, or recyclable. To their surprise, a growing segment of customers have shown a willingness to pay a premium for such products, selecting them over less friendly rival brands.

Major corporations were quick to respond. Directors for environmental affairs, the same as for consumer affairs, have been joining most of the top management teams. By 1990, one hundred percent of Dutch international companies and the majority of German and Japanese companies had a board member entrusted with environmental responsibilities. In some industry sectors CEOs and senior vice presidents devote as much as a third of their time to ecologic issues. Young managers entering corporate executive suites have a different mind-set from the older generation of managers: Social and environmental factors are an integral part of their business sense.

More and more companies are undertaking costly alterations in product design and manufacturing to meet self-imposed ecologic standards. Executives realize that if their company is to appear environmentally friendly, they must not only sell "friendly" products, but must think about the way those products are manufactured and also about the way they are used by the customer. In consequence companies that sell drinks in recyclable bottles have begun to provide bottle banks for their customers, detergent manufacturers have started to analyze the ecological impact of their product right through their life-cycle, and even suppliers are now screened for good environmental records. America's three leading tuna canners decided that their fish must be caught in "dolphin-friendly" ways, a British retail chain insisted that the beef it sells must not have grazed on deforested Brazilian pastures, and a Canadian grocery retailer determined to put only "green" products on its shelves. As a result of a growing number of such moves, a whole new industry has been arising, dealing with biodegradable and organic products, environmentally harmless substances, the recycling of reusable materials, and the cleanup of existing pollution. This "Earth Age Industry" employs more than 200,000 people in the United States alone.

The Paradigm Shift in Science. The contemporary sciences, physics and cosmology above all, have known several "revolutions" in our time, starting with Einstein's relativity revolution at the turn of the century. The latest revolution is particularly profound. Its seeds were sown in mid-century, but they came to flower in the last ten to fifteen years. This revolution concerns the way scientists view the world. The gist of it is that the world is not like a giant *mechanism,* as it was in classical mechanics, but rather like a vast *organism.* As in an organism every part affects every other, so in the natural universe every atom, every galaxy, has an effect on every other atom and every other galaxy.

The shift in what has become known as the "paradigm" of

THE CHANGING VISION OF SCIENCE

The Old	The New
A system is completely reducible to its elements: "the whole is the sum of its parts."	The whole system is irreducible to its parts—it has emergent properties in regard to the properties of the parts.
All things can be analyzed to simple causes, and all causes and effects are distinguishable.	Processes within systems have multiple causes, and causes and effects are not rigidly distinguishable (what was a cause can become an effect, and vice versa).
There are no intrinsic purposes (programs, if given, are externally inputted).	Systems have intrinsic goals (behavioral or developmental "programs" and tendencies).
Parts are intersubstitutable; exchanging them does not change the properties of the whole.	Parts are not substitutable without changing the properties of the whole system.

science is affecting the kind of knowledge that scientists produce, and therefore the kind of technologies that are spun off from scientific knowledge.

The technological spin-offs of science are well known: The miracle of electronics, lasers, instant worldwide communication, automated production, biotechnology, and their ilk are highly visible. But it is just as important to recognize that the worldview that underlies these technological marvels is very different from that which generated the lever and the steam engine. Within new disciplines and scientific frameworks—

(continued from page 188)

The Old	**The New**
Parts are externally related (what one part *is*, is not determined by its relations)	Parts are mutually constitutive (what each part *is* depends on its relations to all other parts).
Boundaries are clearly definable (objects and environments are separable).	System boundaries are fuzzy (known only by step functions in energy, matter, and information exchanges between the system and its milieu).
Organizational levels in systems are clearly distinguishable and hierarchically related.	Organizational levels are interpenetrating and heterarchic (systems function by multiple decision centers rather than top-down commands).

such as cybernetics, general system theory, nonequilibrium thermodynamics, Big Bang cosmology, nonlinear dynamics, general evolution theory, and theories of chaos and self-organization—scientists are developing an organically unified vision of reality.

Gaining a unified picture of the world has always been the ambition of poets and philosophers. In our day hard-nosed natural scientists are busy elaborating unified theories. In their emerging concept, human beings are as much a part of nature and cosmos as the greatest galaxy and the smallest atom.

The social sciences are changing as well: They manifest growing interest in the connections that bind individuals not only to economic and political but also to ecologic and cultural structures and processes. Since the late 1980s even august disciplines, such as neoclassical economics, have been descending from the ivory tower of higher mathematics to consider the effect of environmental degradation and global change on the way people produce and consume, and make decisions in private and professional spheres.

Increasingly, university courses deal with the interface between economics, society, and nature. Environmental economics is becoming a recognized discipline. Also new publications are appearing on the scene, for example, *Environmental Economics* and *Ecological Economics,* the latter published by an international society of that name in existence since 1989.

The public resonates to the new paradigm of science. Stephen Hawking's *Brief History of Time* sold more than a million copies; James Gleick's *Chaos: Making of a New Science* made the best-seller lists. In 1990 one large Manhattan bookstore devoted an entire window to new books on physics and cosmology; another displayed Paul Davies' *The Cosmic Blueprint* next to the latest collection of Garfield cartoons. The editor of a popular science book series declared that we are entering the golden age of science.

Reinterpretation in Religion. Changes are occurring also in the domain of religion. There is a veritable spiritual renaissance in many parts of the world, with people young and old exploring fresh approaches to ancient doctrines or coming up with new concepts. Within university circles a new theology is being articulated: It attempts to bring classical dogma into harmony with science. Leading theologians realize that the cosmologies promulgated in science provide a normative context that could guide and energize society. The new worldviews and cosmologies of science could tell us what the world is, how it has evolved, and where it is heading. There is a growing recognition that the new scientific paradigm, replacing the mechanistic with the organistic worldview, could become a source of creativity and spirituality for humanity.

Traditional creation stories were mythic and symbolic, yet they not only narrated the cosmic order but prescribed how it applies to order here on earth. As above so below: All things had their proper place. Today's cosmology is the work of physical and life scientists, but they do not tell people how to act, or even why. Theologians such as Thomas Berry consider it their mission to fill this lack.

Berry said that we are in trouble because we do not have a "good story." The Old Story, the classical account of how the world came to be and how we fit into it, is not functioning properly, and we did not yet learn a New Story. Theologians and humanists hope to come up with one. In their reinterpretation the processes of the universe are spiritual-psychical, not only material-physical. They are highly integrated, forming an inclusive whole of which humans are a part. The human body had its origins in primordial atoms, and mind and spirit originated there, too. Ever since, they have been shaped by the overarching processes of evolution in the cosmos.

In the New Story the universe is not a cosmic layer cake with its many levels created at the same time. Rather, the cosmos evolved from shared material-spiritual origins, with the higher levels emerging out of the lower through self-transcendence. Today, after 15 billion years of material-spiritual evolution, human beings have a chance to set forth this creative unfolding consciously and purposively. It is in us that the evolving

universe achieves self-recognition. It is our primary sacred community. Recognizing the sanctity of all creation we could move,
as Albert Schweitzer suggested, from the uncaring exploitation of our environment toward a true reverence for nature.

The new theology offers a reinterpretation of the nature of
the divine. It contests the idea that God is external to His (or
Her) creation. This view is replaced with the concept that God
is immanent throughout the universe. A divine spirituality is
intrinsic to all things, from atoms to humans. Human beings it
inspires from within, rather than commanding from above.
Such a concept, part and parcel of non-Western spiritual traditions, is not foreign to Christianity: It is there in the naturalism
of St. Francis of Assisi, as well as in the evolutionism of Jesuit
biologist Pierre Teilhard de Chardin.

The New Story tells us that the evolutionary forces at work
in the cosmos are also at work in our psyche. We can recover
them by getting in touch with our innermost spirituality. In
this way we can achieve a fresh sense of kinship with nature, a
deeper sense of human origins. We can come to the insight that
to act responsibly in this world we need to understand our
deeper selves. The immanence of the divine in an organically
evolving material-spiritual universe could revitalize society,
and provide guidance for all of us.

Society is in ferment. New movements are emerging in profusion: eco-feminism, deep-ecology, eco-philosophy, environmental education, animal rights. Thousands of organizations
are becoming active, translating the emerging social, ecologic,
corporate, scientific, and spiritual insights as practice-oriented
social, economic, ecologic, and political projects.

There are more and more "green" movements; an increasing number of institutions dedicated to appropriate and
alternative technology; and a mushrooming of organizations
championing sexual rights, the conservation of cultural and
ethnic traditions, and native and tribal cultures, to mention
but a few. In the industrialized world action-oriented organi-

zations such as Amnesty International, the Worldwide Fund for Nature, Greenpeace, and Earth First! are motivating public opinion and spurring political action, while in the southern hemisphere liberation theologies are acquiring power, combining the prophetic tradition of the Bible with the traditional concerns of Socialism.

These are signs of hope in the contemporary world. There is resilience and creativity in the human spirit. Faced with shocks and crises, people do not lapse into passive pessimism or hold fast to obsolete ideas. They strike out to explore new paths of thought and action. The challenge facing us is to ensure that the new values and ideas do not remain on the level of insight, but find practical application. Changing visions and values, and the practices that flow from them, must begin to penetrate government policy, corporate strategy, and consumer choice, as well as citizen behavior.

11

The Evolutionary Future

Our generation, of all the generations in history, is called upon to decide the destiny of life in this corner of the universe. The choice is ours: evolution or extinction.

The choice is not academic. We now have the technology and the power to terminate human life, and indeed almost all life, on this planet. We could reach this catastrophic outcome either by the fast route of a nuclear holocaust or by the slower path of a continued degradation of the life-supporting environment. Nobody would consciously choose either one of these routes, but they could be taken just the same: through ignorance, carelessness, and the persistence of obsolete images, values, and practices.

We could also choose evolution. This choice merits further thought.

The choice of evolution presupposes that we have succeeded in meeting the current imperatives of perception and action. This means that we have acquired a critical measure of evolutionary literacy; learned to replace intercultural coexistence with interexistence; managed to catalyze the necessary degree of social creativity; adopted global, moral, and responsible ways of thinking and living; provided access to the necessary forms and levels of education, information, and communication to people; and succeeded in creating a functional and reasonably equitable world order.

All this makes for a tall order but an imperative one. If it is met, the new world would not develop as a continuation of the present, nor would it head toward global breakdown or global dictatorship. A functional framework would be created for the survival and development of the whole family of peoples and nations on this planet. The evolutionary scenario could unfold. *What would it be like?*

Many people look at the future as if the world of tomorrow would be basically the same as today's world, only everything would be bigger and better. People will travel by automated highways in fast and supersilent luxurious vehicles, from robotized homes where they have only to utter a wish to have it carried out by ever-present computers, to automated factories and offices where, in addition to supervising the smart machines that carry out most of the tasks of manufacturing and administration, they need only to make some executive decisions. Nobody will have to work for more than thirty hours a week and for more than eight years of his or her life; everyone will have the rest of a ninety-plus-year lifespan to enjoy the many facets of leisure and recreation.

How people will spend their leisure time sets off the above "superindustrial" from the "postindustrial" image of the future. In the superindustrial future people ride ever more cars and planes, make ever bigger deals, and produce to the utmost limit of their strength and possibilities. In the postindustrial future they also have the miracles of technology at their command, but they prefer to use them to engage in social and cultural activities, undertaking creative pursuits, experiencing art and perhaps the variety of virtual realities that will replace television in the home.

Although no super- or postindustrial future could guarantee warm and loving personal relationships, in the postindustrial variant people have good chances to achieve such relationships. Computers match each person with the best-adapted soul mates, companions, and spouses, and everyone has the time to enjoy one another's company, as well as the communities that grow around such rationally developed relationships.

A technological super- or postindustrial future may be

abhorrent to a few of us, but it is likely to sound good to most people. We can save our breath arguing its merits: This is not the real-world scenario that is in store for humankind. There is a basic physical element that, combined with a likewise basic socioeconomic factor, blocks its realization. The physical element is the inability of the planet, in terms of its energy, material, space, and ecologic resources, to sustain or even bring about the required level of resource consumption for all but a small minority of people. Of course, on an optimistic technological view, this blockage is not irremediable. We will tap the energy of the atom and of the sun, recycle wastes, and if necessary colonize the sea bottom and outer space.

However, such optimism misses the socioeconomic factor—the world's social and economic constraints. We now have one-fourth of the world population in the advanced industrialized countries and three-fourths in the poverty-stricken under-developed world, including China. By the time a high-tech future can materialize, the one-fourth of the world's people who can bring it about will shrink to one-tenth. Can one-tenth of the world population move into a technological super- or post-industrial paradise, while nine-tenths are quagmired in the pre-industrial stage?

Even if we could improve on the iron curtains of the past and seal our borders with laser screens so that poverty-stricken migrants cannot penetrate them (as Germany contemplates doing along its Eastern frontier), we could not seal our technological installations against terrorism. And we could never seal our air and our water, and our cities, lands, and forests against the waves of pollution that would roll over them from a 90-percent underdeveloped human population. The Scenario 2 we have outlined in Chapter Nine must inevitably shift into Scenario 1.

Leaving the socioeconomic reality of the world out of account makes for a slide into unrealistic utopias. Evidently, if the industrialized countries move toward the superindustrial stage, the developing countries would have to move toward the industrial stage. (Unless they could leapfrog it entirely; that, however, given current levels of education and preparedness, is not likely.) The presently poor majority of humankind would have to graduate to a better form of existence: It would have to cease polluting and exploiting the environment, and it would have to improve its lot sufficiently so as to not want to migrate to greener pastures. In turn, the privileged minority would have to cut down on its own, currently still excessive rates of resource consumption and waste, clean up and safeguard its environment, and generally desist from acting in ways that would foreclose the options for life and development of the majority. All this is colossally unlikely indeed.

In the final analysis it is a diversified yet integrated world, and not a super- or postindustrial utopia, that is the evolutionary future available to us. Our world is diverse, both in the values and perceptions of people and in the level of development attained by societies; and these diversities will not disappear overnight. They will not disappear even in the course of the twenty-first century. In the foreseeable future the only uniformity we could realistically impose on our world is the uniformity of poverty, resulting from overcrowding and overexploitation.

The evolutionary future is not less desirable for embracing diversity. Diversity gives us the variety that is justly regarded as the spice of life. Even more important, it offers alternatives, and hence safeguards in the event that we find ourselves in blind alleys that would lead to developmental dead ends.

In the world of the evolutionary future, some people and societies will live on a higher technological plane than others. They can do so in good conscience, provided that they do not rob others of the chance to develop according to their values and priorities. Noncoercive development, guided by a globally concerned morality, can allow some populations to move into the postindustrial stage, and others to enter the industrial one. The discrepancy will not breed resentment and conflict. There is sufficient regard by people and societies for one another not to play off their own interests against those of others, whether they are bystanders, competitors, or presumed adversaries. Instead, they prefer win-win games in which the gain of one is also the gain of the others.

The evolutionary future is not a technological utopia, but neither is it a violence-prone and eco-degraded dystopia. It is a world where some societies develop highly advanced technology, offering comfort, mobility, and productivity, with efficiency in the use of precious energy and material resources and the cleanup and recycling of wastes. It is a world where other societies evolve in different ways, guided less by material and technological and more by social and spiritual goals and ideals. They put lesser emphasis on the industrial availability of natural resources, and more on harmony with nature.

A world of this kind would be diverse, but not inequitable and unjust. It could satisfy the genuine needs of all people, and it could be indefinitely sustainable. Will it be the world of our future? This depends only on us. On our timely choice between evolution and extinction.

Afterword

Federico Mayor
Director-General of UNESCO

The Choice makes disturbing reading from various crucial perspectives. It would be difficult to deny the troubling trends Laszlo lays out as the possible sources of a future none of us would freely wish to inhabit. Pressures of population growth, of our impact on the oceans and atmosphere, of humanity's more and more fragile grip on the food chain are all issues that should occupy the top of our community agendas. Yet these questions, so closely bound up with the drama of poverty, rarely become salient in the marketplace of political ideas or, more important, on our timetables for action.

If, in fact, the roots of what Laszlo calls the "fifth wave" lie in obsolete beliefs, we owe current change in such beliefs more to the global shock wave of overpopulation, poverty, environmental degradation, global warming, and other trends, than to our own prescience. After all, Rachel Carson wrote of the *Silent Spring* almost forty years ago, and indications of ozone layer depletion were first noted in the early seventies. Thus, if events are rapid and indeed accelerating, we as citizens of the global community have moved far too slowly to capture trends upstream. We seem perennially caught in the dynamic of catching up with events, rather than setting an agenda that places us ahead of them.

Our century, as Laszlo correctly suggests, began with pioneering breakthroughs into nonlinear, nonmechanistic constructs of nature and of human nature. As H. Stuart Hughes showed in *Consciousness and Society,* the turn of this century marked the turning away from Newtonian and social Darwinist models toward the insights of Einstein on relativity and of Freud and Jung on the hidden sources of our own personalities. The two, of course, converge in the sense that seeing clearly and thinking clearly require a degree of self-knowledge and a capacity for growth that transcends academic specialization or years of political experience.

We are indeed shamefully slow to internalize the dramatic injustices that go on around us and, inevitably, threaten the quality of our lives. It is not in the abstract but in the concrete that, I believe, we can find the sparking points of new perceptions—of seeing the extraordinary in what we have been desensitized to accept as the ordinary, natural order of things. The points of rebellion that will permit us to surf the fifth wave involve "lightning flashes of insight" in which our ethical core is touched by unnecessary poverty and suffering, easily avoidable ignorance and extremism, and ill-adapted structures of perception and decision-making that keep us from seeing the trends that may well erupt in our local communities and our private lives.

Examples abound of our emotional and intellectual distance from the "facts of life" around us. The net shift of wealth in the world is not from the richer to the poorer countries, but the reverse: About $60 billion flow yearly from South to North to meet debt payments and to pay for goods. The brain drain continues to deprive the poorest countries of their greatest hope for development: trained scientific and professional personnel. The same phenomenon threatens the fragile democracies of Eastern and Central Europe. Without the investment and human resources needed for development, without development based on the cultural needs and social values of their people, Third-World countries could continue to slide into deeper poverty and instability. The greatest population shift of our times has been from countryside to city, with growing numbers choosing better opportunities to school their young, more accessible health facilities, and paid jobs, even if these in-

volve shantytown living for tens of millions of new urban immigrants. Who, then, will farm the land, provide the food, and
tend nature?

Even in the wealthier countries, education systems are in
crisis, young people sense a loss of direction and purpose, and
the epidemics of drugs and AIDS continue to grow. Environmental problems recognize no boundary between nation or region, no barrier between rich and poor. The military threat of
nuclear holocaust seems to be receding, yet the peace divi-
dend, including the application of the military's advanced
technical and manpower capacities to civilian problems, seems
far down on the community agenda. In all of these matters, a
sense of drift, of waiting prevails. This is merely a way of visiting a more difficult, less habitable world on our children and
their children.

These are the everyday realities of our modern lives. Yet
our specializations, our inward turning to private concerns,
our seeming safety in the bureaucratic and institutional structures of work and leisure, shield us from the need to act—and
to act quickly.

The first point of rebellion will be against the prejudices
we harbor within ourselves. And the most important prejudice
is the whispered litany of posterity telling us that things are as
they are because they were meant to be that way. This is the
voice of "common sense" that lulls our reason and our sense
into accepting the world around us as given. This kind of na-
ively optimistic fatalism would have us believe that things have
worked out fairly well so far and, therefore, that nothing too
terrible can happen further down the road.

Less than two decades into this century, Western Euro-
peans descended from the gilded age into the trenches of the
First World War. The most educated generation in history me-
chanically marched out from the trenches to die by the tens of
thousands in the "crash and thunder of the Somme." The so-
called Great War set off shock waves that continue to mark
many aspects of present-day politics. Simple answers to complex questions formed the ideological base not only of the

obvious extremes, but of political discourse in mass society. The results have hardly been satisfactory, from the perspective of either the natural scientist or the political scientist.

Leadership, on the other hand, requires a sharing of complexity with the community and a summons to grapple together with problems that have no easy answers. This is as true in the primary school classroom as it is in the lecture theater of a university. It is all too rare in the political arena. Great teaching, like outstanding political leadership, requires the patience and courage to question the present, to debunk slogans and lay out the immense range of choices available to free and self-motivating individuals.

As long as the local, short-term, and narrow immediate comforts predominate, the voice of impatient truth and of beckoning dreams will be muted, and action will be painfully slow to come. That is why *The Choice* poses uncomfortable questions and seeks new and more rapid solutions. This is a challenge that each of us and each of our institutions must confront if the evolutionary scenario for our future is not to collapse into a full-scale retreat and decline.

Education, from our earliest, formative years through the length of our lives is, as Laszlo shows, the answer: learning to develop infinite and distinctive creative capacities; learning to care about our common heritage, both national and international; learning to share not only what each of us has received and accomplished, but also what is more important and yet untouched—our shared future. It is not only with common threats and fears that we can succeed, but with common ethical principles: educational and cultural sharing that breaks down barriers to perception, forges new attitudes toward other human communities and toward nature, creates an opening for a pro-active attitude to our shared future. These are modalities that can provide more active citizens and more decisive leaders. This was the hope of UNESCO's founders; it is the hope that retains that combination of vision and pragmatism that can take us beyond the fifth wave and on to an evolutionary future.

Selected Writings on Evolution and Society

I. STANDARD AND RECENT WORKS
(in alphabetical order)

Abraham, Ralph, and C. Shaw. *Dynamics: The Geometry of Behavior.* Santa Cruz: Aerial Press, 1984.

Ashby, W. Ross. *An Introduction to Cybernetics.* London: Chapman & Hall; New York: Barnes & Noble, 1956.

Beer, Stafford. *Platforms of Change.* New York: John Wiley & Sons, 1979.

Beishon, J., and G. Peters. *Systems Behavior.* New York: Open University Press, 1972.

Bertalanffy, Ludwig von. *General System Theory: Essays on Its Foundation and Development.* [rev. ed.] New York: George Braziller, 1968.

Blauberg, I. V., V. N. Sadovsky, and E. G. Yudin. *Systems Theory: Philosophical and Methodological Problems.* Moscow: Progress Publishers, 1977.

Boulding, Kenneth E. *Ecodynamics, a New Theory of Societal Evolution.* Beverly Hills and London: Sage, 1978.

Bowler, T. Downing. *General Systems Thinking: Its Scope and Applicability.* New York: Elsevier North Holland, 1981.

Buckley, Walter, ed. *Modern Systems Research for the Behavioral Scientist.* Chicago: Aldine, 1968.

Cavallo, Roger E., ed. *Systems Research Movement: Characteristics, Accomplishments, and Current Developments.* Louisville, KY: Society for General Systems Research, 1979.

Chaisson, Eric J. *Cosmic Dawn: The Origin of Matter and Life.* Boston: Atlantic, Little, Brown, 1981.

Checkland, Peter. *Systems Thinking, Systems Practice.* New York: John Wiley, 1981.

Churchman, C. West. *The Systems Approach.* (rev. and updated) New York: Harper & Row, 1979.

Club of Rome, Council of. *The First Global Revolution.* (written by Bertrand Schneider and Alexander King) New York: Pantheon Books, 1991.

Corning, Peter A. *The Synergism Hypothesis: A Theory of Progressive Evolution.* New York: McGraw-Hill, 1983.

Csányi, Vilmos. *General Theory of Evolution.* Durham and London: Duke University Press, 1989.

Davidson, Mark. *Uncommon Sense: The Life and Thought of Ludwig von Bertalanffy.* Foreword by R. Buckminster Fuller. Introduction by Kenneth E. Boulding. Los Angeles: J. P. Tarcher, 1983.

Demerath, N. J., and R. A. Peterson, eds. *System, Change and Conflict.* New York: Free Press, 1967.

Eigen, Manfred, and P. Schuster. *The Hypercycle: A Principle of Natural Self-Organization.* New York: Springer, 1979.

Eisler, Riane. *The Chalice and the Blade: Our History, Our Future.* San Francisco: Harper San Francisco, 1987.

Eldredge, Niles. *Time Frames.* New York: Simon & Schuster, 1985.

Eldredge, Niles, and Stephen J. Gould, "Punctuated Equilibria: An Alternative to Phylogenetic Gradualism," in Schopf, ed.: *Models in Paleobiology.* San Francisco: Freeman, Cooper, 1972.

Falk, Richard, Samual S. Kim, and Saul H. Mendlovitz, eds. *Toward a Just World Order.* Boulder, CO: Westview Press, 1982.

Foerster, Heinz von, and George W. Zopf, Jr. *Principles of Self-Organization.* Oxford and New York: Pergamon Press, 1962.

Fuller, Buckminster. *Operating Manual for Spaceship Earth.* Carbondale: Southern Illinois University Press, 1970.

Gharajedaghi, Jamshid. *Toward a Systems Theory of Organization.* Seaside, CA: Intersystems Publications, 1985.

Glansdorff, P., and I. Prigogine. *Thermodynamic Theory of Structure, Stability and Fluctuations.* New York: Wiley Interscience, 1971.

Gray, William, and Nicolas Rizzo, eds. *Unity Through Diversity.* (2 vols.) New York: Gordon & Breach, 1973.

Haken, Hermann. *Synergetics.* New York: Springer, 1978.

Haken, Hermann, ed. *Dynamics of Synergetic Systems.* New York: Springer, 1980.

Handy, Charles. *The Age of Unreason.* Boston: Harvard Business School Press, 1990.

Henderson, Hazel. *Paradigms in Progress.* Indianapolis, IN: Knowledge Systems, Inc., 1992.

Jantsch, Erich. *Design for Evolution.* New York: Braziller, 1975.

———. *The Self-Organizing Universe.* Oxford: Pergamon Press, 1980.

Jantsch, Erich, and Conrad H. Waddington, eds. *Evolution and Consciousness.* Reading, MA: Addison-Wesley, 1976.

Katchalsky, Aharon, and P. F. Curran. *Nonequilibrium Thermodynamics in Biophysics.* Cambridge, MA: MIT Press, 1965.

Katsenelinboigen, Aron. *Some New Trends in System Theory.* Seaside, CA: Intersystems Publications, 1984.

Klir, George J., ed. *Trends in General Systems Theory.* New York: Wiley-Interscience, 1972.

Koestler, Arthur, and J. R. Smythies, eds. *Beyond Reductionism: New Perspectives in the Life Sciences.* London and New York: Macmillan, 1969.

Margenau, Henry, ed. *Integrative Principles of Modern Thought.* New York: Gordon & Breach, 1972.

Maturana, Humberto R., and Francisco Varela. *Autopoietic Systems.* Biological Computer Laboratory, University of Illinois, Urbana, IL: 1975.

Nappelbaum, E. L., Yu A. Yaroshevskii, and D. G. Zaydin. *Systems Research: Methodological Problems.* U.S.S.R. Academy of Sciences, Institute for Systems Studies. Oxford and New York: Pergamon Press, 1984.

Nicolis, G., and I. Prigogine. *Self-Organization in Non-Equilibrium Systems.* New York: Wiley Interscience, 1977.

Pattee, Howard, ed. *Hierarchy Theory: The Challenge of Complex Systems.* New York: Braziller, 1973.

Prigogine, Ilya, and I. Stengers. *Order Out of Chaos* (La Nouvelle Alliance). New York: Bantam, 1984.

Rapoport, Anatol. *General System Theory: Essential Concepts and Applications.* Cambridge, MA: Abacus Press, 1986.

Salk, Jonas. *The Anatomy of Reality.* New York: Columbia University Press, 1984.

———. *The Survival of the Wisest.* New York: Harper & Row, 1973.

The Science and Praxis of Complexity. Tokyo: The United Nations University, 1985.

Senge, Peter M. *The Fifth Discipline.* New York: Doubleday, 1990.

Simon, Herbert A. *The Sciences of the Artificial.* Cambridge, MA: MIT Press, 1969.

Thom, René. *Structural Stability and Morphogenesis.* Reading, MA: Benjamin, 1972.

Weiss, Paul A., et al. *Hierarchically Organized Systems in Theory and Practice.* New York: Hafner, 1971.

Whyte, L. L., A. G. Wilson, and D. Wilson, eds. *Hierarchical Structures.* New York: American Elsevier, 1969.

Wiener, Norbert. *The Human Use of Human Beings: Cybernetics and Society.* (2nd ed.) Garden City, NY: Doubleday Anchor Books, 1954.

Zeeman, Christopher. *Catastrophe Theory.* Reading, MA: Benjamin, 1977.

II. SELECTED BOOKS BY THE AUTHOR
(in chronological order)

Essential Society: An Ontological Reconstruction. The Hague: Martinus Nijhoff, 1963.

Individualism, Collectivism and Political Power: A Relational Analysis of Ideological Conflict. The Hague: Martinus Nijhoff, 1963. (also in Japanese)

Human Values and Natural Science. (edited with J. Wilbur) New York and London: Gordon & Breach, 1970.

Evolution and Revolution: Patterns of Development in Nature, Society, Culture and Man. (edited with R. Gotesky) New York and London: Gordon & Breach, 1971.

Introduction to Systems Philosophy: Toward a New Paradigm of Contemporary Thought. New York and London: Gordon & Breach; Toronto: Fitzhenry & Whiteside, 1972. Reprinted: Gordon & Breach, 1984; second edition: New York: Harper Torchbooks, 1973.

The Systems View of the World: The Natural Philosophy of the New Developments in the Sciences. New York: George Braziller, 1972; Toronto: Doubleday Canada, 1972; Oxford: Basil Blackwell, 1975. (also in Persian, Japanese, French, Chinese, Korean, and Italian)

The Relevance of General System Theory. (edited) New York: George Braziller, 1972.

Emergent Man. (edited with J. Stulman) New York and London: Gordon & Breach, 1972.

A Strategy for the Future: The Systems Approach to World Order. New York: George Braziller, 1974. (also in Japanese and Korean)

The World System: Models, Norms, Applications. (edited) New York: George Braziller, 1974.

Goals for Mankind: A Report to the Club of Rome on the New Horizons of Global Community. New York: E. P. Dutton, 1977; Toronto & Vancouver: Clarke, Irwin, 1977; London: Hutchinson, 1977; revised edition: New York: New American Library Signet Books, 1978. (also in Italian, Spanish, Finnish, Japanese, and Serbo-Croatian)

Goals in a Global Community, Vol. I: Studies on the Conceptual Foundations. (edited with J. Bierman) Oxford and New York: Pergamon Press, 1977. *Vol. II: The International Values and Goals Studies.* (edited with J. Bierman) Oxford and New York: Pergamon Press, 1977.

The Inner Limits of Mankind: Heretical Reflections on Contemporary Values, Culture and Politics. Oxford and New York: Pergamon Press, 1978; revised edition: London: Oneworld Publications, 1989. (also in German, French, Italian, Chinese, and Korean)

The Objectives of the New International Economic Order. (with R. Baker, E. Eisenberg, and V. K. Raman) New York: UNITAR and Pergamon Press, 1978; reprinted 1979. (also in Spanish)

The Obstacles to the New International Economic Order. (with J. Lozoya, J. Estevez, A. Bhattacharya, and V. K. Raman) New York: UNITAR and Pergamon Press, 1979. (also in Spanish)

The Structure of the World Economy and Prospects for a New International Economic Order. (edited with J. Kurtzman) New York: UNITAR and Pergamon Press, 1980. (also in Spanish)

Disarmament: The Human Factor. (edited with D. F. Keys) Oxford and New York: Pergamon Press, 1981.

Systems Science and World Order: Selected Studies. Oxford and New York: Pergamon Press, 1984.

World Encyclopedia of Peace. Volumes I, II, III, IV. (edited with Linus Pauling and Jong Y. Yoo) Oxford: Pergamon Press, 1986.

Evolution: The Grand Synthesis. Boston and London: Shambhala New Science Library, 1987. (also in Italian, German, Chinese, Spanish, Portuguese, and French)

The New Evolutionary Paradigm. (edited) New York: Gordon and Breach, 1991.

The Age of Bifurcation: The Key to Understanding the Changing World. New York and London: Gordon & Breach, 1992. (also in German, Spanish, Chinese, French, and Italian)

The Evolution of Cognitive Maps: New Paradigms for the 21st Century. (edited with I. Masulli) New York: Gordon & Breach, 1993.

A Multicultural Planet: Diversity and Dialogue in Our Common Future. Report of an Independent Expert Group to UNESCO. (edited) Oxford: Oneworld, 1993. (also in German)

The Creative Cosmos: A Unified Science of Matter, Life, and Mind. Edinburgh: Floris Books, 1993. (also in French, Italian, German, Portuguese, and Chinese)

Vision 2020. New York and London: Gordon & Breach, 1944.

Index

About the Author

Ervin Laszlo, Ph.D., author of twenty-seven books and editor of twenty-eight anthologies, including *Goals for Human Society: A Report to the Club of Rome on the New Horizons of Global Community; Evolution: The Grand Synthesis;* and *The Creative Cosmos: A Unified Science of Matter, Life, and Mind.* He is advisor to the Director-General of UNESCO, rector of The European Academy for Evolutionary Management and Applied Studies, founder and director of The General Evolution Research Group, and director of Planetary Citizens. He is president of The Budapest Club, a prominent member of The Club of Rome, editor of *World Futures: The Journal of General Evolution,* and associate editor of *Behavioral Science.* Dr. Laszlo was Professor of Philosophy at the State University of New York, and has taught Systems Science, Futures Studies, World Order Studies, and Aesthetics at Portland State University, the University of Houston, Princeton, and Indiana University. He has been a Fellow of Yale and a Visiting Professor at various universities in Europe and the Far East. He received a doctoral degree from the Sorbonne and honorary doctoral degrees from the Turku School of Economics and Management and the Saybrook Institute, San Francisco. He resides in Montescudaio, Tuscany, Italy.